KENDAL

THROUGH THE AGES

Norman Holloway

AMBERLEY PUBLISHING

ACKNOWLEDGEMENTS

The author would like to express his gratitude to everyone who was interested enough to purchase the first book, and all those who have been keenly awaiting the production of this second book.

Many thanks to the Trevor Hughes collection for the use of almost all the old pictures, and for his assistance in checking all the historical descriptions.

Thank you to everyone who has given large or small pieces of interesting information, and especially those who have kindly allowed me to enter their home or business property in order to capture the present-day pictures.

And finally, I would like to thank my wife Ilene and son Clive, who have tirelessly checked my grammar and punctuation, and the rest of my family who have endured having to be the subject in some of the pictures.

I could not have done it without you, so thanks!

First published 2014

Amberley Publishing
The Hill, Stroud, Gloucestershire, GL5 4EP
www.amberley-books.com

Copyright © Norman Holloway, 2014

The right of Norman Holloway to be identified as the Author of this work has been asserted in accordance with the Copyrights, Designs and Patents Act 1988.

ISBN 978 1 4456 1840 1 (print)
ISBN 978 1 4456 1847 0 (ebook)

British Library Cataloguing in Publication Data.
A catalogue record for this book is available from the British Library.

Typesetting by Amberley Publishing.
Printed in Great Britain.

INTRODUCTION

This second book of comparison photographs has been produced as a result of the unexpected success of the first book, *Kendal Through Time*, published in 2012.

In *Kendal Through The Ages*, the interesting format of the original book has been adhered to with a complete series of different pictures. Some of the subjects may be similar but all the photographs are completely different, with one or two of them previously unseen.

Booksellers Waterstones took such great interest in book one that it appeared in their 'Kendal Top Ten Chart' for a number of weeks, and was at one stage their number one bestseller in the Kendal shop.

I was also pleased that *The Westmorland Gazette* gave such an excellent book review (written by Allan Tunningley), which included a very interesting full-page feature along with some of the pictures from the book.

Once more, I have tried to recreate the modern pictures as close as I could to the original photographers' position, which again was not always easy, and in a couple of places almost impossible.

The finished format, as before, takes a complete tour of the town, with some small detours here and there, but always returning to the main route of the journey.

I hope that I have pointed out things along the way that may not have previously been known to the reader and, as a result, they will be able to wander the streets of Kendal looking at the area from a brand new perspective and with a greater interest in this lovely old town.

My main appreciation must go to all those Kendalians who, like myself, love this town and its fascinating past – so much so that their kind comments regarding book one made this second edition something that just had to be done.

I hope you enjoy it!

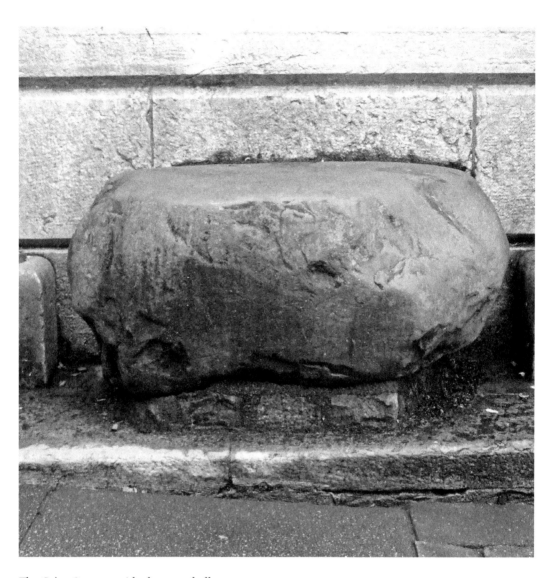

The Ca'an Stone outside the town hall.

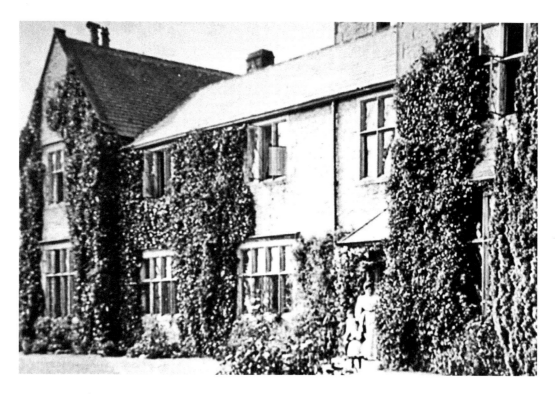

Howard Home

Howard Home was established initially as an orphanage for young girls in 1865 by Mary Howard of Levens Hall; the road outside was even known locally as Orphan's Home Hill. Its use was completely reversed in the 1950s when it became a home for the elderly. Later it was used to accommodate refugees from the war in Bosnia, until in 1996 it was finally converted into a hotel by hotelier Tom Harwood of Windermere.

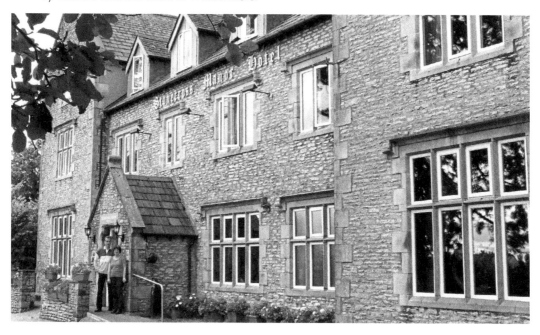

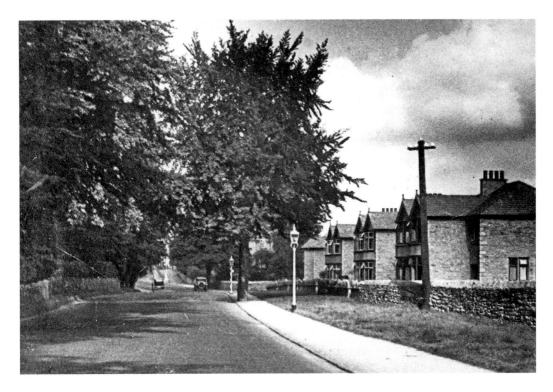

Milnthorpe Road

On the back of the original of this old picture was written the date '8th August 1935', which coincides with the construction of these houses by local builders Howies of Kendal in the same year. In the distance, Vicarage Terrace can be seen. Behind the wall to the left was Hawesmead House, owned by G. F. Braithwaite (six times mayor), which was unfortunately destroyed by fire and had to be pulled down. The road was widened when the new bridge at Romney Road was built.

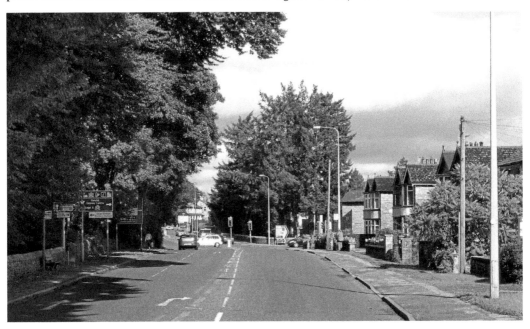

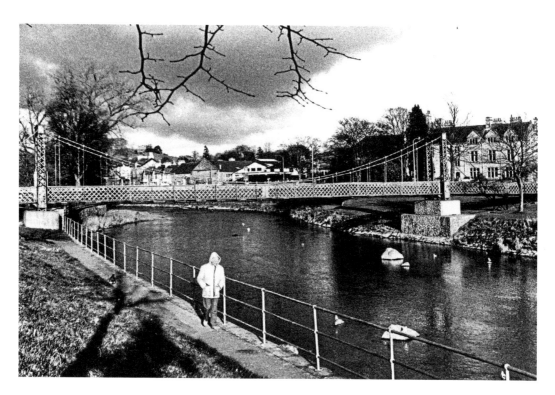

Romney Road Bridge

The old wooden Romney Road suspension bridge was removed when the new road bridge was built in 1992 to improve motorised access across the river. The old bridge was flooded to the wooden deck level in the 1954 flood and, as a result of the Lancashire River Improvement Scheme in the 1970s, there has been no significant flooding since. The old bridge has been resited between Dockray Hall and the Mintsfeet Industrial Estate.

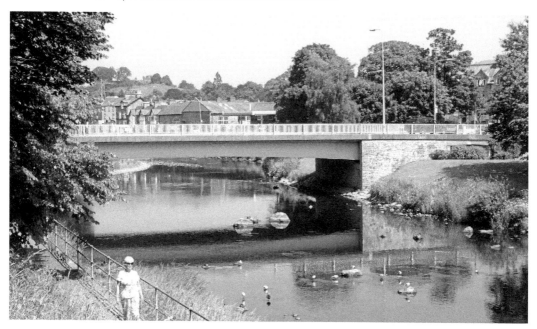

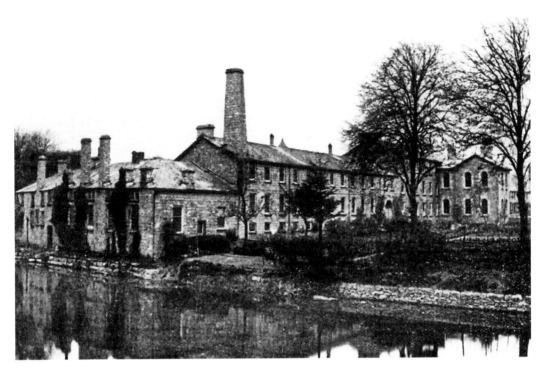

Netherfield Works

This is an early picture of the River Kent and Netherfield Works (named after the land upon which it was built) before it was extended into the vast buildings that later dominated Lound Road. The property was finally demolished in 2000 to make way for the new K Village shopping complex. The gabled building to the right was the rear of what was to become the main entrance to the works. Notice that behind the tree on the far right, the houses on Parkside Road can be seen.

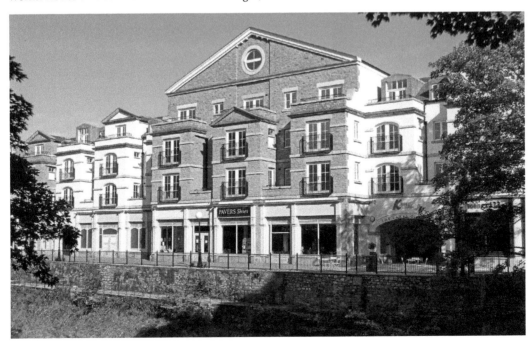

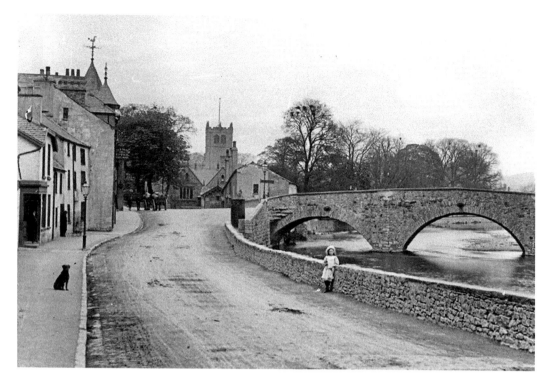

Nether Bridge

Nether Bridge was originally the only access into Kirkland and Kendal from the south, as Milnthorpe Road in earlier days was merely a winding track. The first stone bridge was very narrow and had to be widened on two further occasions, in 1772 and 1908, to accommodate the increase in horse and motorised traffic. Under the bridge, as shown inset, can be seen the three different types of construction methods used at the times.

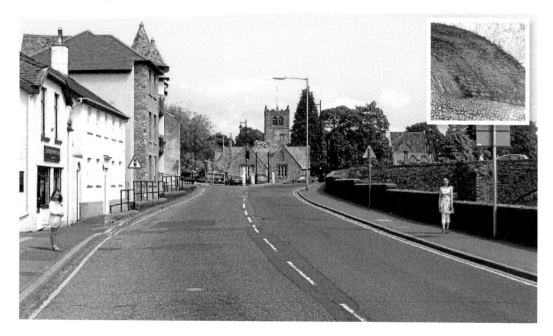

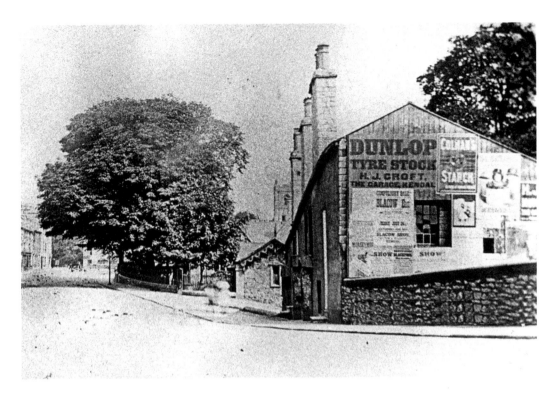

Malt Kiln Cottages, South Side

This is a view of the Malt Kiln Cottages not often seen, looking at them from the south. The only two things that remain are the stone wall to the side of Nether Bridge and the parish church bell tower. It is interesting to note the advertising on the building for tyres at H. J. Croft's garage in Highgate and for a sale at Blacow Bros. In today's picture, notice the hand-painted town crest among the flower beds.

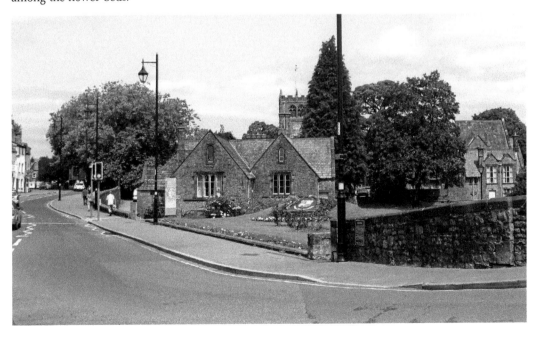

10

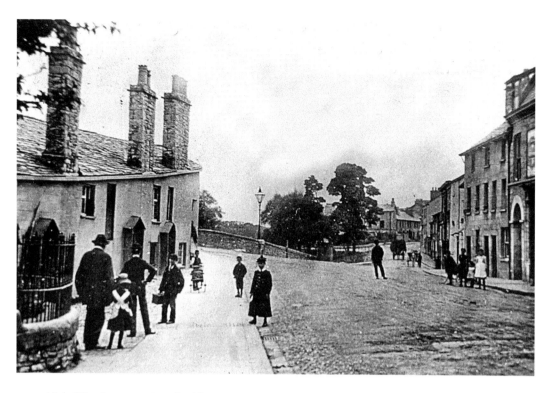

Malt Kiln Cottages, North Side

The cottages on the left stood on the Kirkland side of Nether Bridge, next to the old ford and Glebe Cottage. The buildings were removed in 1906 and the area has been landscaped ever since. The properties on the right have also seen some changes, especially the property behind the girl in white, which was derelict for many years. Notice the tower of the former Cock & Dolphin public house is not in the old photograph.

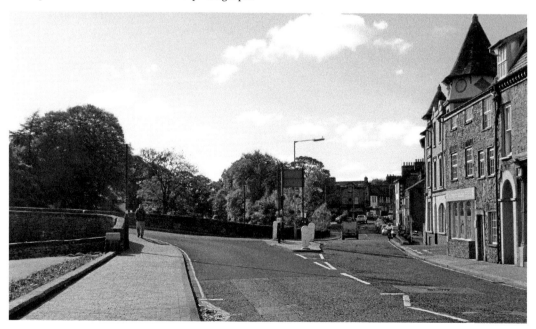

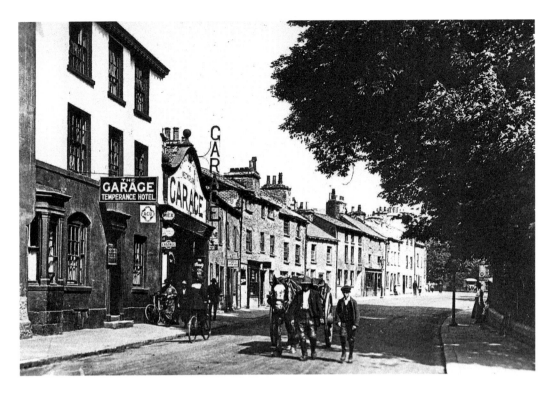

Kirkland Garages

Here we have an old view looking north in Kirkland showing Atkinson & Griffin's Garage, the first of a number of such businesSes to operate on this site. This property had various owners before its final proprietor, G. B. Bedford. It is now part of Kent Court retirement apartments. The buildings behind the horse were later to become Crabtree's Garage, which has now been developed into housing and retail. The car in the distance on the far right is outside the Ring O' Bells public house.

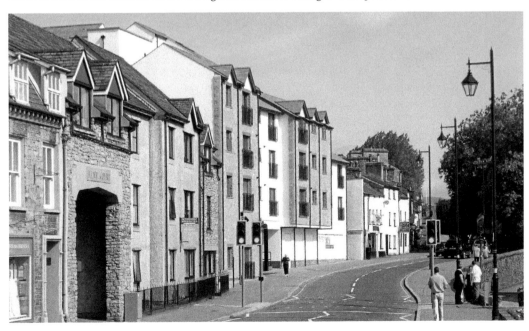

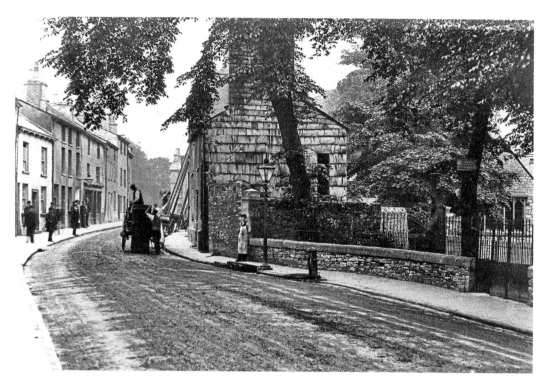

Kirkland, 1904

The old picture shows the preparations for the demolition of the buildings just south of the parish church to make way for a car park. Beyond the ladders can be seen the end of the Ring O' Bells public house. In today's picture, the Kirkland Hall, over to the right, still remains and the buildings between the two pedestrians on the left have also survived. The one-way system of 1968 still causes traffic problems in this historic area at peak times.

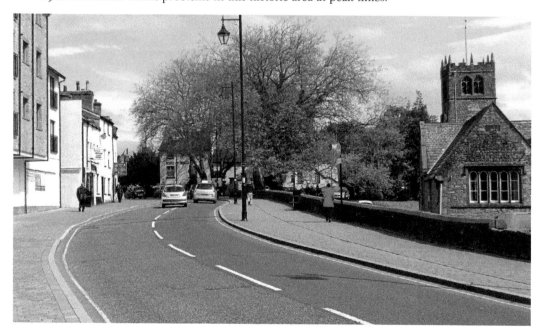

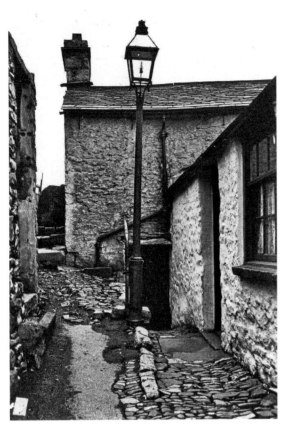

Kirkbarrow Lane

This lane has a very narrow access from Kirkland opposite the parish church, next to the Wheatsheaf public house. It used to lead past the now demolished Kirkbarrow House to the still standing Anchorite House. The lane is clearly shown on John Todd's map of 1787. As can be seen in today's picture, some of the cottages in the lane are still in use. Nowadays, the lane leads into the Kirkbarrow estate (the name meaning 'church burial ground'). Kirkbarrow Lane was recently a much discussed item in the letters page of *The Westmorland Gazette*, regarding the use of a little known nickname for it – 'The Crack'.

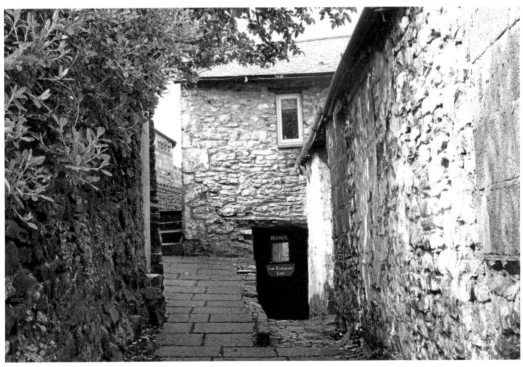

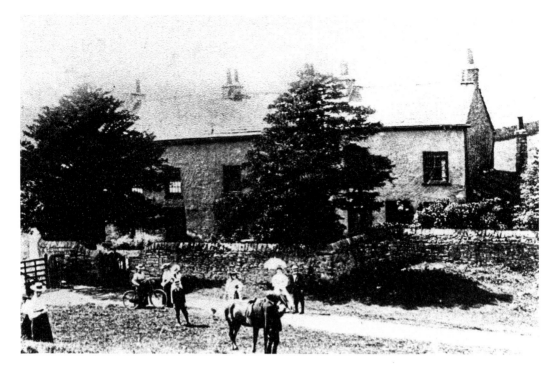

Anchorite House

On this religious site over a thousand years ago lived a hermit. It is claimed that even before Christianity the spring leading to the well, which is said to never run dry, was probably a site of pagan worship. Around the sixth century St Mary's chantry was built here, its work being taken over by Kendal parish church in the thirteenth century. On Speed's map of 1614, a previous property is shown as 'The Ankerite'; the present-day house was built in 1771.

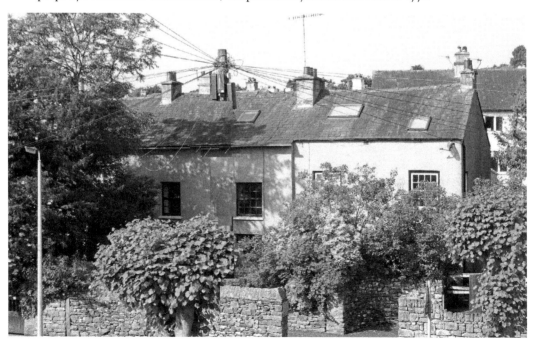

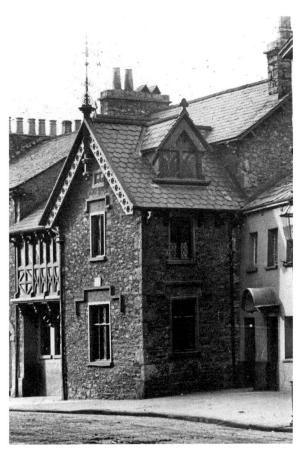

Old Kirkland

In this old part of Kendal, the building in the centre is dated 1563 and is now 450 years old. The old picture shows the rough road prior to being tarmacked, with horse droppings. This area of the town has hardly changed at all, apart from the modern habit of painting the walls in lighter colours. Notice the old weather vane is still in place above the decorative gable. A sign of the times is the television aerial attached to the chimney stack in the modern-day picture.

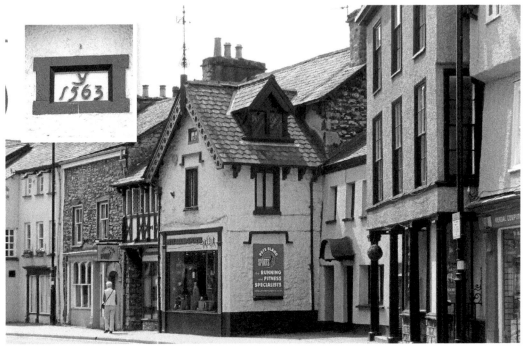

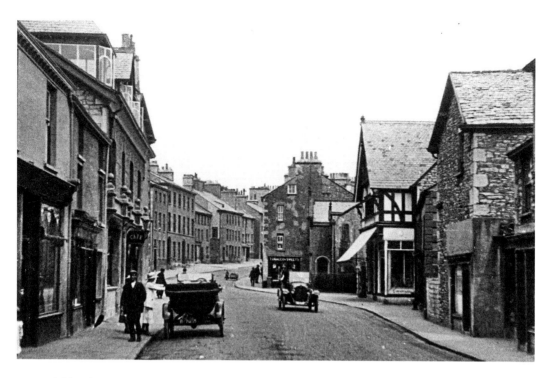

Kirkland, 1920

This wonderful old picture shows just how little Kirkland has changed in almost 100 years. Behind the approaching car, to the right, is the now demolished Dowker Hospital. In the modern-day picture, many of the buildings, even The Highgate Hotel in the centre distance, have brightly painted external walls. The removal of the roof windows on the property to the left is the only structural change to the scene, though two-way traffic is a thing of the past.

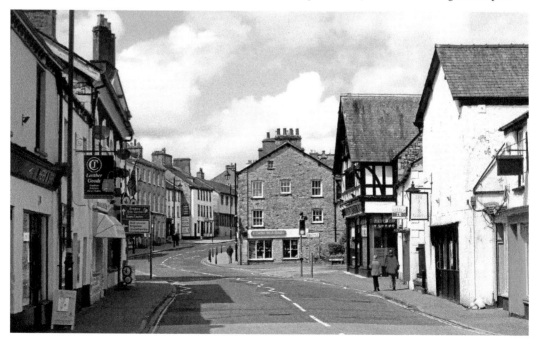

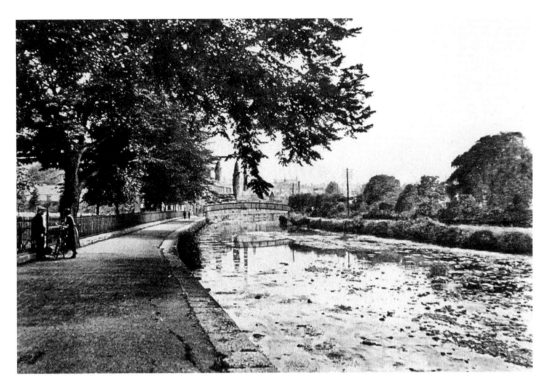

Colonel's Walk

This walk was named after Col. George Wilson, who lived in Abbot Hall. Notice the railings around the park, removed during the Second World War to aid in the manufacture of armaments; however, there are none at the edge of the river, which would be unthinkable in today's safety-conscious world. A nice reflection of Jennings' footbridge can be seen in the old picture, along with the ending of the mill race on the right before the river was widened.

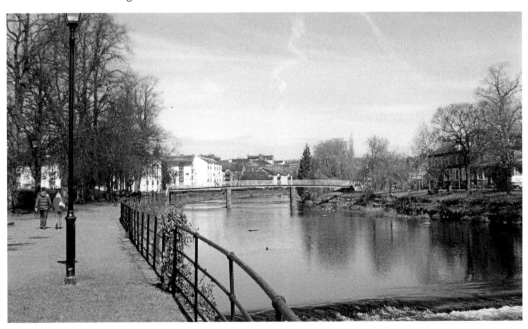

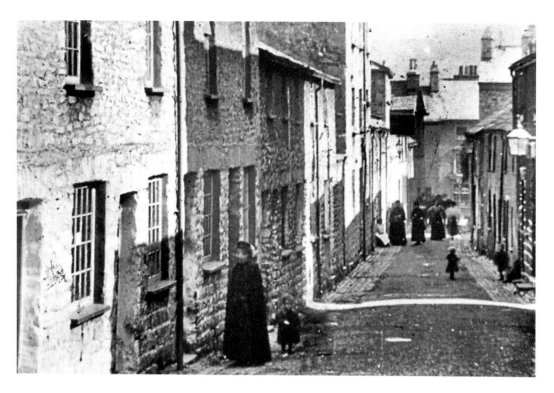

Captain French Lane

This street was earlier called Ratten Row but was renamed after a Royalist officer, who once lived at the bottom of the lane. The buildings here are still recognisable today. The large buildings on the left have been used by local undertakers Hayes & Parkinson since 1892. Notice in the old picture a shaft of light coming from the early morning sun in a very narrow Buttery Well Lane, as well as the wall-mounted gas lamp on the right.

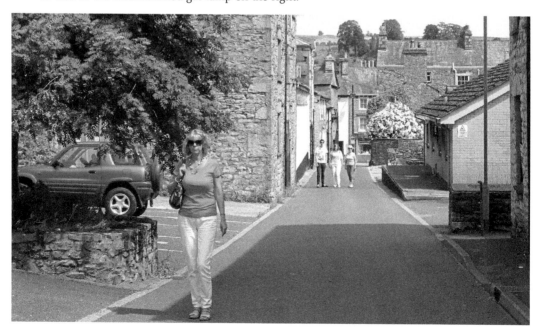

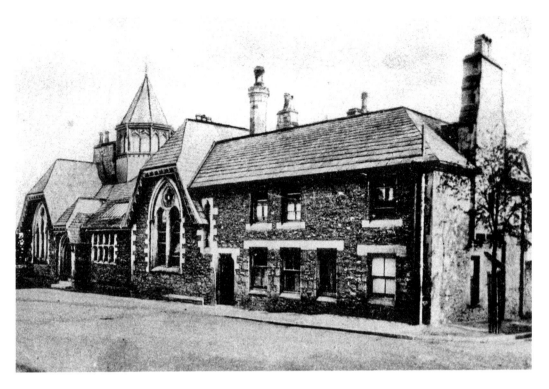

Cropper Memorial Hospital

This hospital, with room for eighteen patients, was built in 1869 by James Cropper (the last MP for Kendal) as a memorial to his wife, who died when their daughter Mary was only eighteen years old. A children's ward was later added in 1873 and the building is now fittingly used as a children's nursery. It was replaced in 1907 when the much bigger Westmorland County Hospital was built across the road.

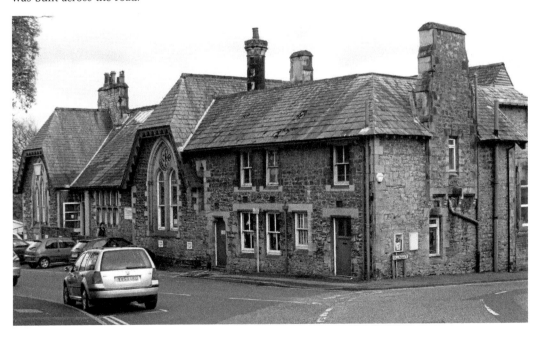

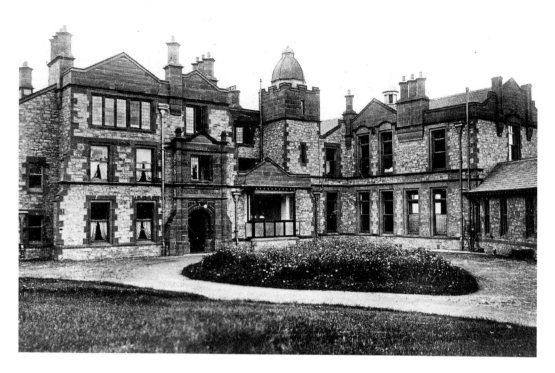

Westmorland County Hospital

The Westmorland County Hospital, built at a cost of £15,200, was opened in 1908. When it was converted, after almost ninety years, into the Summerhill Nursing Home, the building incorporated a dome and clock from the original hospital, but the clock has since been stolen. A new hospital, known as The Westmorland General Hospital, was built on Burton Road in 1989 and opened in 1991.

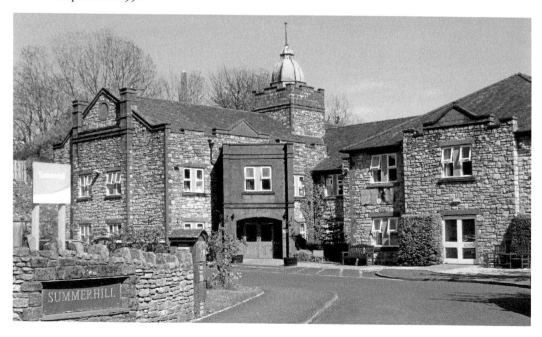

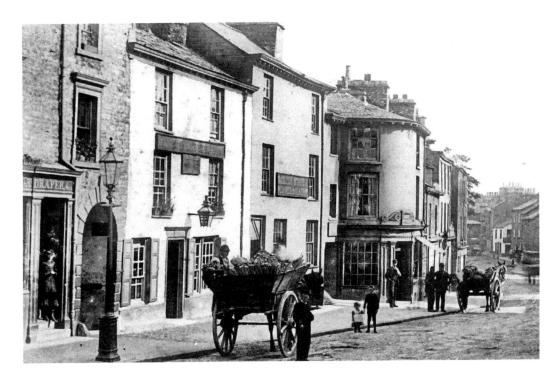

The Bishop Blaize

The Kendal Bowman public house was previously named The Bishop Blaize (after the patron saint of wool trade workers). The name was changed to the Kendal Bowman around 1960, but the yard behind the lamp on the left in the old photograph is still called Bishop's Yard. After being empty for a number of years, it has now been restored and converted into residential accommodation. An interesting feature is the retention of what is believed to be the Vaux Brewery crest.

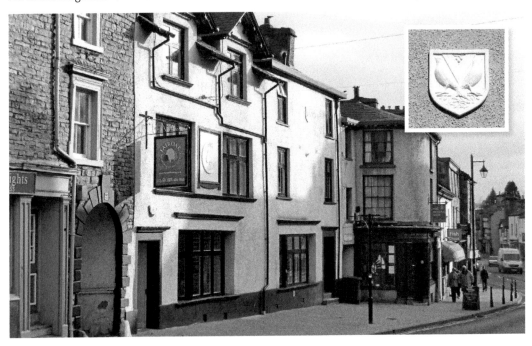

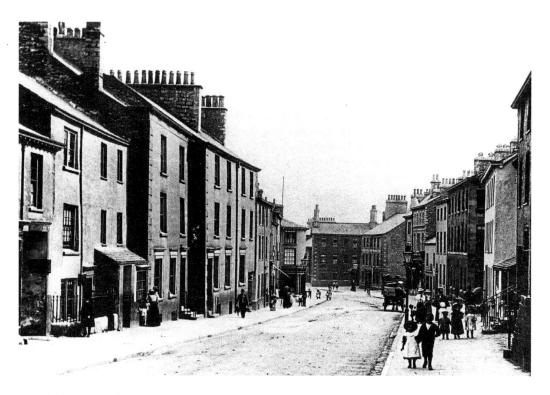

Highgate Bank

This picture looks down Highgate from near the Brewery Arts Centre entrance. Yard 131 is just visible on the left and in the centre distance is the former Queen's Hotel, which for a time in the 1990s became a nightclub. The hotel appears not to have changed, but a separate building on the north side near Gillinggate has been removed. On closer inspection, I have managed to count as many as twenty-six children in the old picture – you may find even more.

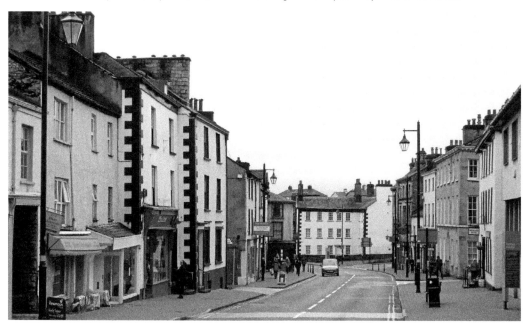

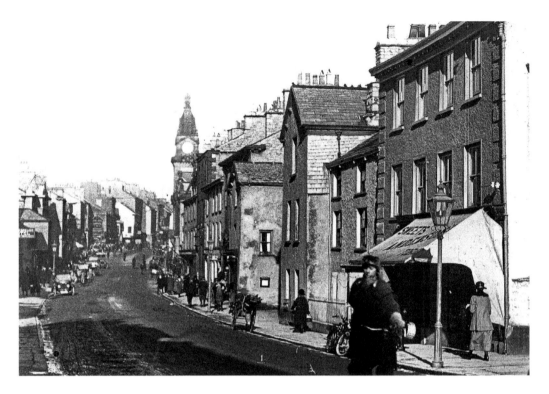

Highgate

In this old view of Highgate the building on the right is Andersons' Sweets & Tobacco shop, later The Bookworm and now Rug Emporium. In the gap to the right of the window cleaner's cart is the entrance to Dr Manning's Yard. Notice that the buildings of the Auld Grey Town nowadays tend to be mostly white; also compare the vastly different street lighting. The cyclist is riding against today's traffic, but at least he's not on the pavement!

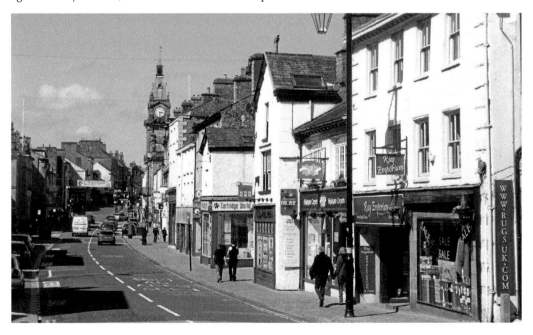

Webster's Yard

Webster's Yard, one of Kendal's newer yards, commemorates the well-known architect Francis Webster, who came to Kendal in 1788. Over the next sixty years, he was architect for some of the finest buildings in the town. Inside this yard can be found the original doorway to the former Dowker's Hospital, which had stood near the entrance to Abbot Hall Park, opposite Gillinggate. The doorway was saved and installed at first-floor level facing Highgate when the yard was constructed in 1988.

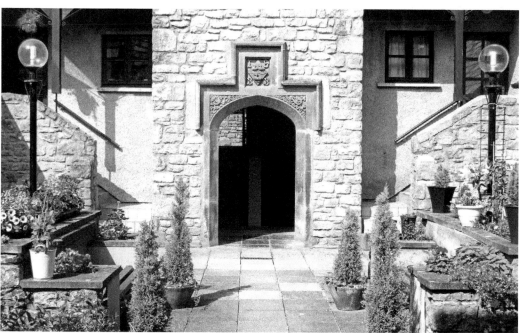

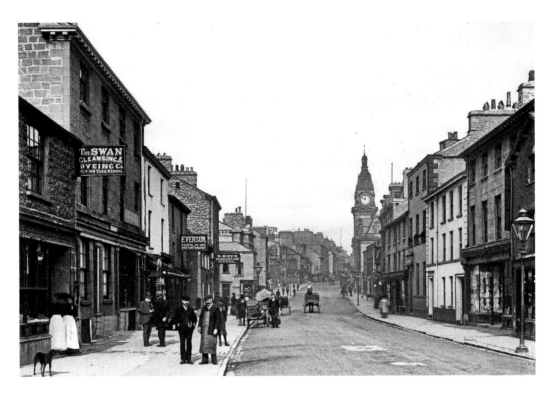

Highgate

This is Highgate before the days of the motor car, which is much in evidence in today's picture. The larger building on the left would, in later years, become the business premises of H. J. Croft motor dealers, who began trading in Wildman Street. It is interesting to note that on the entrance floor, in mosaic tiles, can still be seen the words 'MOTORS FOR HIRE'. Until recently, the building was still in use as a clothing store.

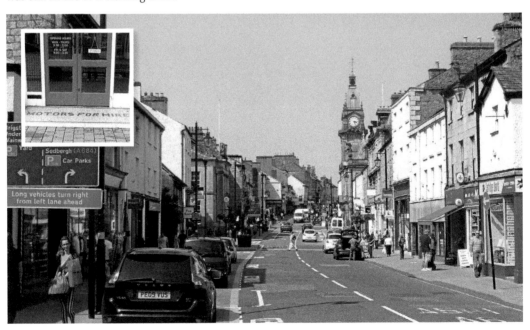

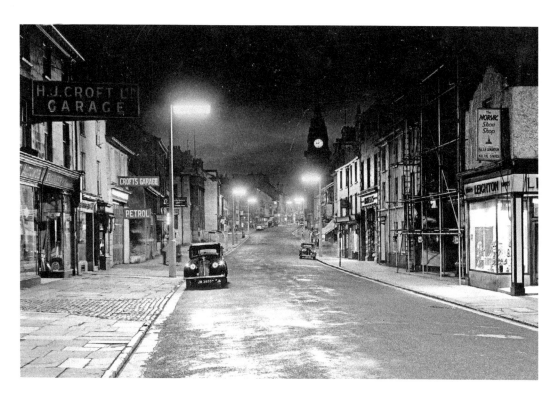

Highgate at Night

This old view of Highgate was taken from outside what used to be called the Marvic Hotel, next door to the New Inn. F. & J. F. Leighton's shoe shop is prominent on the right, with its window lighting switched on. Notice the cars with their parking lights, and there's an eerie quiet to the street, considering the town hall clock is at 9.07 p.m. Compare that to today's picture, taken at 6.10 a.m.

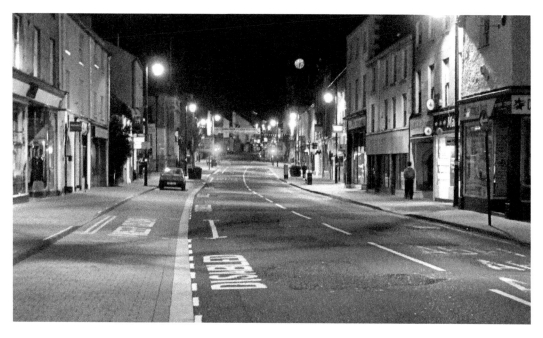

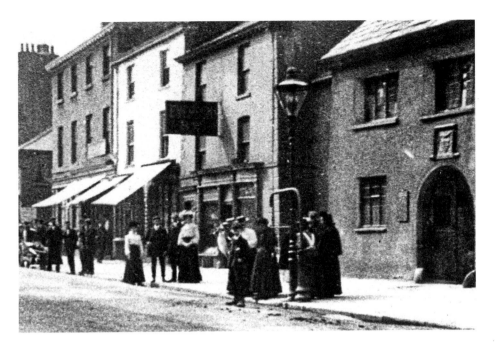

H. J. Croft's

This old picture of Highgate shows only minor changes to the buildings. Next to the ladies standing outside Sandes Hospital is a gas lamp and a water pump used for refuelling the steam vehicles. The property behind the red car in today's picture was originally H. J. Croft's car showroom, while the garage's workshop entrance was at Hollywood Nails. After the garage's closure, and with alterations, the buildings in the centre are now both the same height.

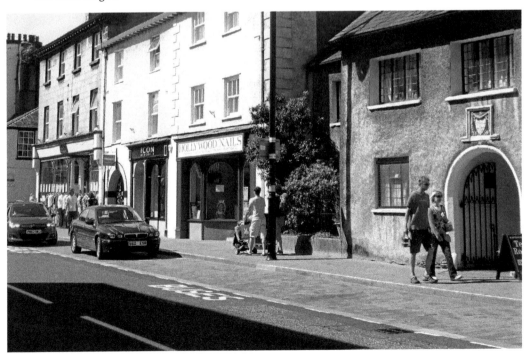

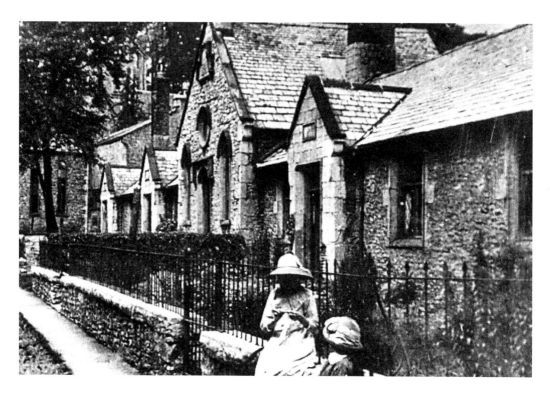

Bluecoat School

The almshouses were built here in 1670 by Thomas Sandes to accommodate eight widows. The entrance to this yard was initially used as a schoolroom and library. The building at the top of the yard, beyond the almshouses, became the Bluecoat School for Boys. By 1714, girls had been allowed entrance to the school. The school continued until 1886, when the school merged with Kendal Grammar School.

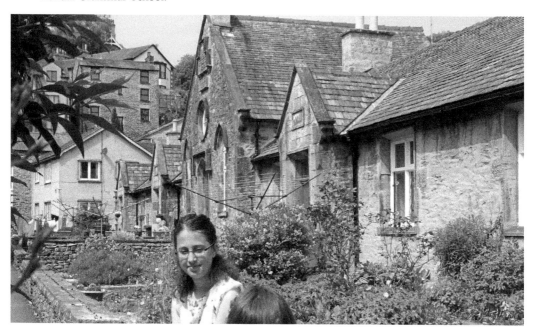

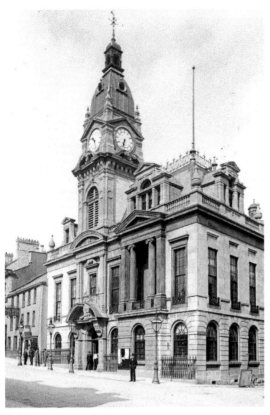

Kendal Town Hall

The town hall building has had this appearance since 1893 when, at a cost of £22,200, it was extended, the clock tower built and the carillon installed. The carillon is unique in that a tune is played every three hours, from 9 a.m., with a different tune for each day of the week. It was first played to celebrate Queen Victoria's Diamond Jubilee in 1897. The clock tower was last renovated in 1999 when large areas of lead were replaced and sections of the stonework renewed. When restored, the four clock faces required a total of 880 sheets of transfer gold leaf. During the renovation, which took many weeks, the clock tower was totally covered in scaffolding and sheeting. Inside the town hall is the council chamber. Although now used for district council meetings, it was previously used as a courtroom, until the new magistrates court was built on Burneside Road and opened by HRH The Princess Royal in 1992. The mayor making ceremony is held in the assembly room. Notice in the old picture that the two clock faces are showing different times.

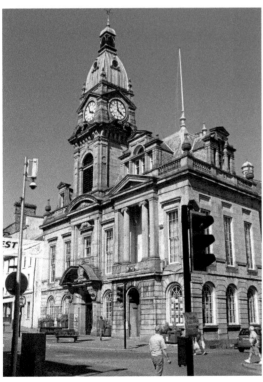

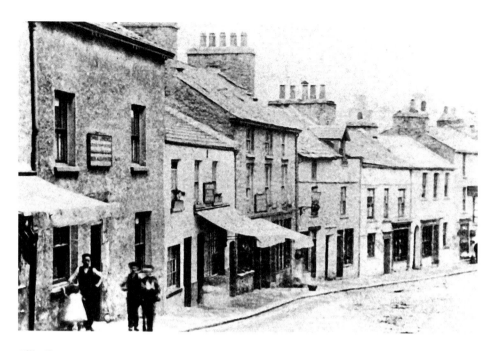

Allhallows Lane

This view looks down Allhallows Lane (formerly Cricklegate) from the junction of Low Fellside and Beast Banks. Once again, as in many scenes of Kendal, there is very little change in appearance, apart from the building centre right, which has gained a dormer window. This street boasted four public houses at one time. Although two closed some time ago, a third one was established when the council offices (previously the public swimming baths) were converted into the Miles Thompson public house, named after the former architect.

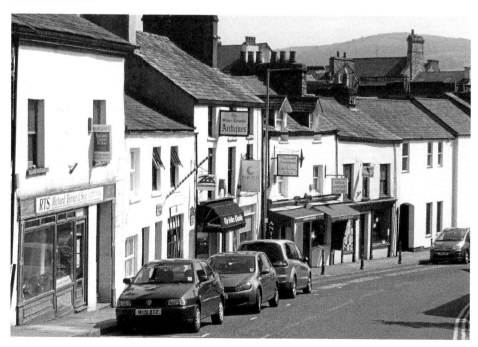

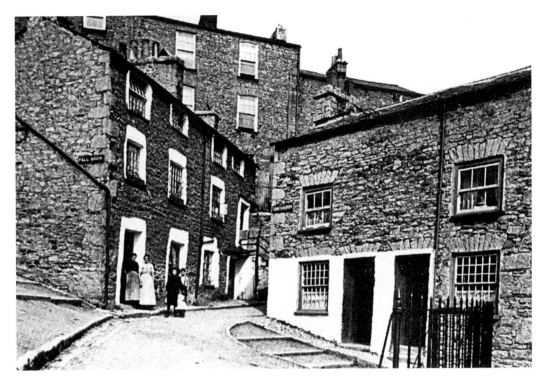

Sepulchre Lane

This old part of Fellside is at the junction of three streets. On the left, coming down from Serpentine Road, is the little known Fell Brow, while going down to the right, leading to the Hyena and Low Fellside, is Fountain Brow. The street in the centre, which also comes down from Serpentine Road (the tall buildings at the rear) and goes down to Low Fellside, is Sepulchre Lane. Most of this area was cleared and modernised in the 1960s.

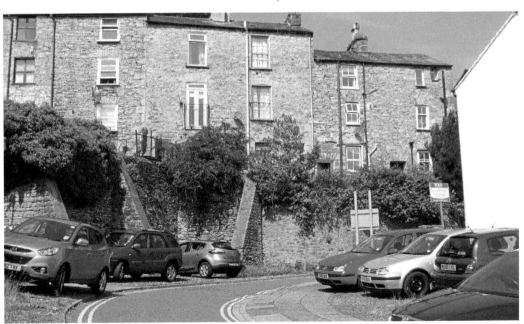

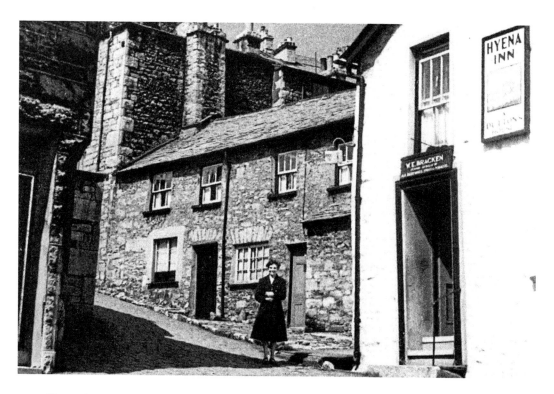

Hyena Inn

The public house, with the handrail and small white lamp on the corner on Fountain Brow, Fellside, was the town's smallest pub, and ceased trading in 1966 after serving local drinkers since 1834. The only clue to its former use is a small signboard over a side door. The buildings on the left still remain, but the family cottages in the centre and the gentle slope have now been replaced by modern houses and wide steps.

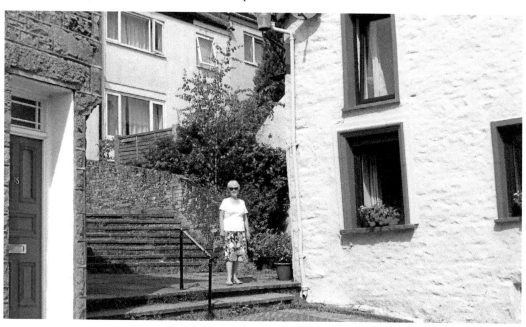

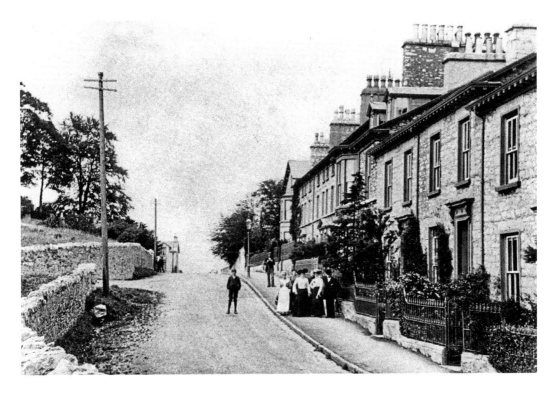

Victoria Terrace

This street, now part of Serpentine Road with Queen's Road bearing off to the left on the brow of the hill, faces High Tenterfell, one of Kendal's many old cloth-drying areas. The trees on the left are at the lower end of Serpentine Woods. An interesting feature in this area is the carvings on the rear gatepost of No. 3 Cliff Terrace, created by John Whatton, a former POW in the Second World War, showing the faces of his four children.

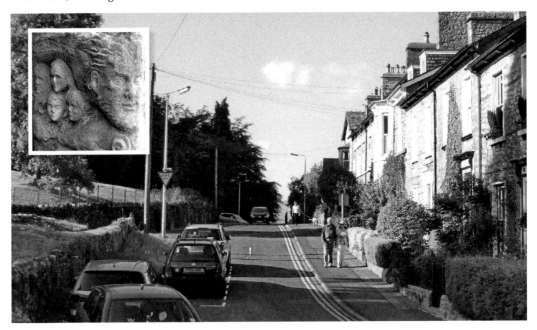

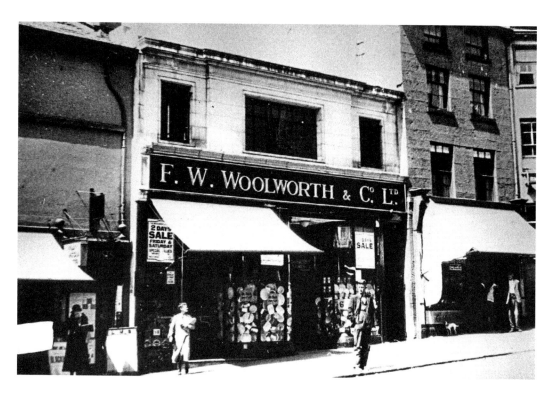

Woolworth's

This is a fine old picture of Kendal's first Woolworth's store, in the days before it took over the business on the right and expanded the building into what it is today. Unfortunately, the company was one of the first to cease business during the difficult trading period in 2005. The author of this book was fortunate to be on the roof of the building to witness the visit of HM The Queen and Prince Philip to Kendal Town Hall in 1956.

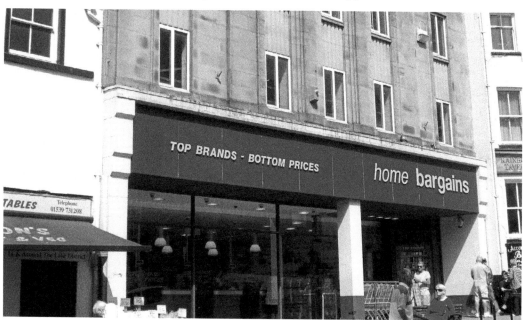

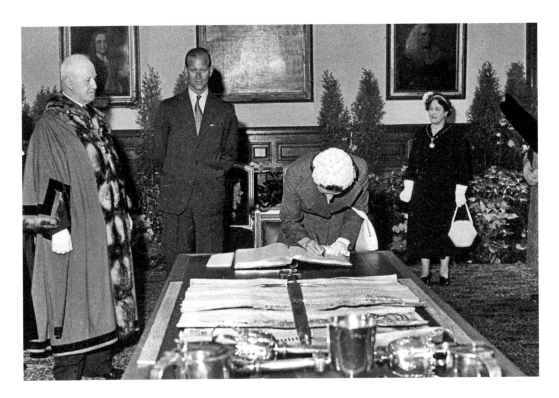

The Mayor's Parlour

Here we have a reconstruction of a photograph showing HM The Queen and Prince Philip in the council chamber at Kendal Town Hall during their visit in 1956. They were greeted by the mayor, Cllr William Gould, and shown many of the town's treasures. The present-day picture, taken in the mayor's parlour, was recreated with the kind assistance of Cllr Sylvia Emmott, the mayor at the time, showing a group of Commonwealth visitors with the same items of regalia as in the earlier picture.

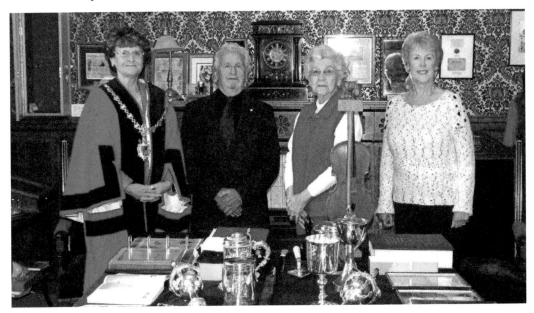

Town Hall Extension

Here we have the town hall looking from the north side, with the new clock tower yet to be constructed. To the left the property of Sinkinson's Wine & Spirit Merchants, which was demolished in 1893 when the town hall was extended. As a result of this work, the frontage of the building was doubled. The arched doorway of the old shop is where the Ca'an Stone is now situated. Notice in the old picture there is a small yard between the two properties, which is where the main entrance is now positioned. In today's picture, the two left-hand windows on the first floor are those of the Mayor's Parlour.

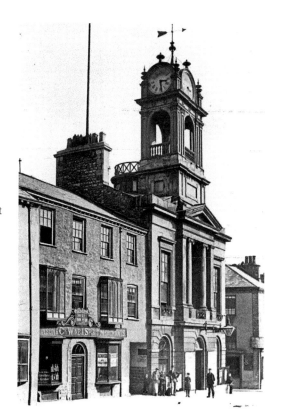

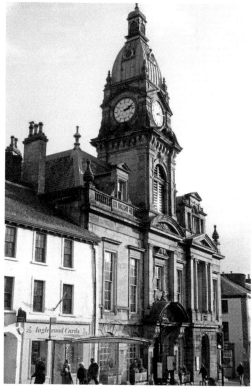

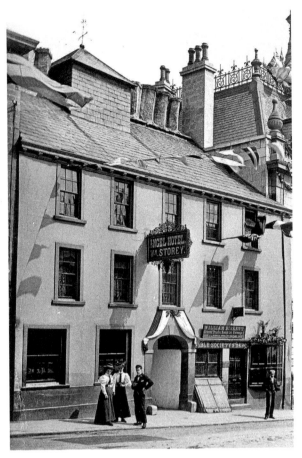

Angel Hotel

The old picture of the Angel Hotel shows it decorated for the celebrations of Queen Victoria's Jubilee. The tiled box shape on the roof was originally used as a dovecote; it is claimed that it was later used for cockfighting. Notice the beer cellar doors under the windows to the Bible Society Department. The area to the left of Angel Yard is now part of the Halifax Building Society. The yard itself, which leads to the South Lakeland District Council offices, had a successful dental practice established here in 2001, later moving further down Highgate. The business still uses the word 'Angel' in its name.

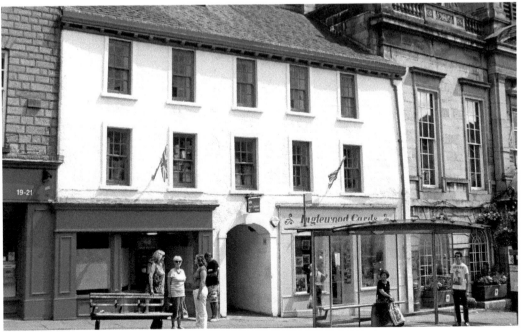

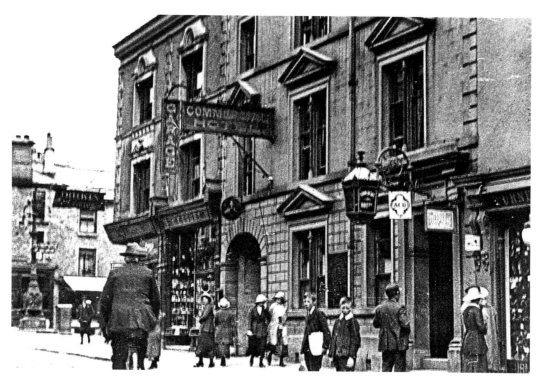

Commercial Hotel

The Commercial Hotel later became known as The Kendal Hotel and was for many years one of the town's most popular wedding venues. It was distinguishable by the fact that the front doors could be altered into a revolving door as the occasion required. Notice in the old picture, the circular sign over the archway for the Touring Car Club. This building is now occupied by one of the many banks in this part of the town.

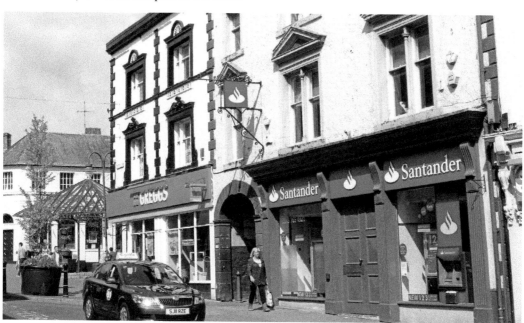

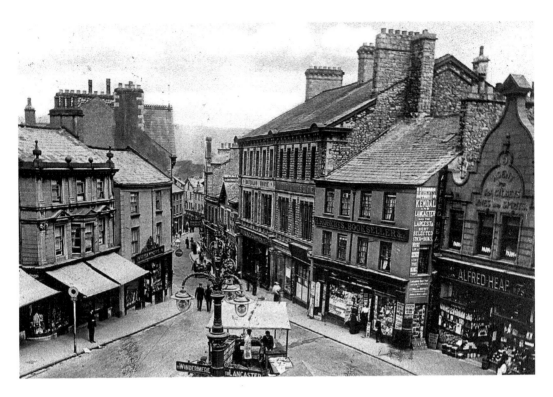

Finkle Street

The ornate lamp post in the centre of the old picture is where today's Birdcage is sited. The building on the right, with the lettering down the side, was the earlier home of Henry Roberts's booksellers before it moved to Stramongate. The large property in the centre used to be Waterloo House, the headquarters of the Kendal Co-operative Society, which had numerous and varied shops in the town. Under the canopy in the centre is what remained of the old fish market.

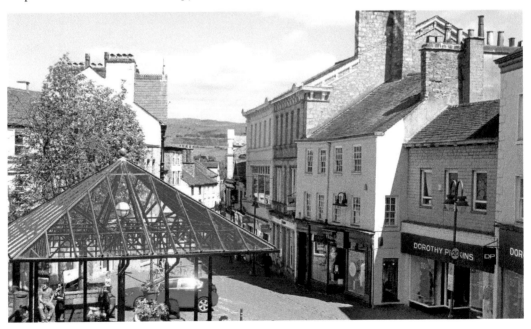

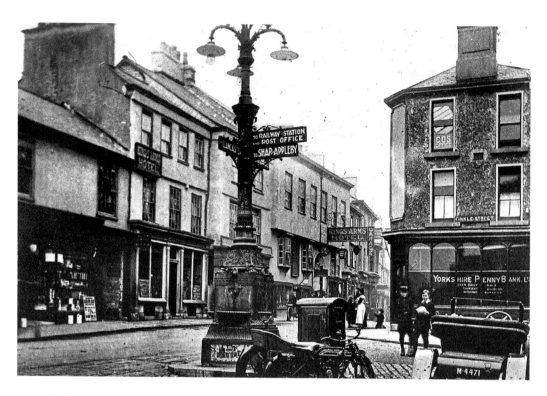

Finkle Street

This is a wonderful old picture taken at the top of Finkle Street. On the right is the Yorkshire Penny Bank, nowadays minus the penny! Notice, where the Birdcage now stands, the direction sign on the lamp post, showing the way to the railway station, post office, Shap and Appleby. The reason for this was that Sandes Avenue was not opened until 1877, and all northbound traffic went down Finkle Street, with the main post office situated in what is now Beales.

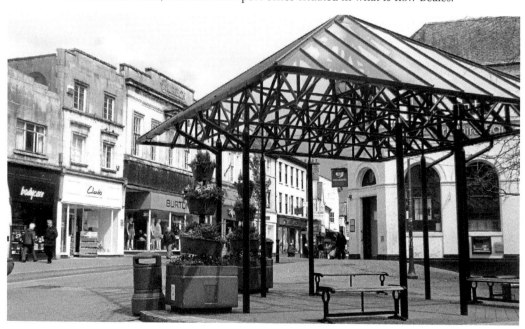

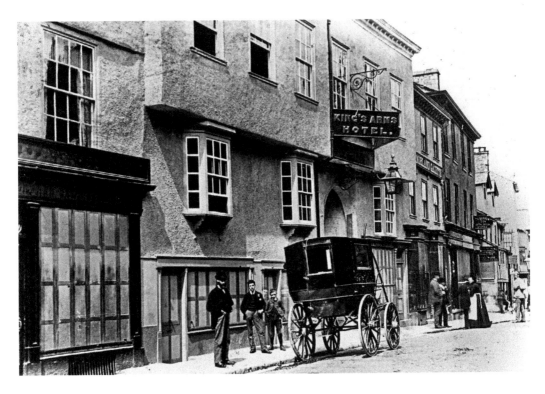

King's Arms Hotel

This picture from 1924 shows the King's Arms Hotel; the archway in the centre would nowadays be the entrance to TK Maxx. On the right were the offices of *The Westmorland Gazette*. The hotel was demolished in 1934 and the area converted into Burton's the tailors and a new Marks & Spencer's store. The latter store moved to the old Webbs' garden nursery site on Library Road, which in the meantime had been redeveloped to accommodate the new Fine Fare store.

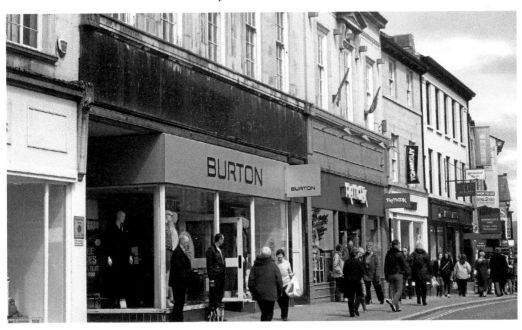

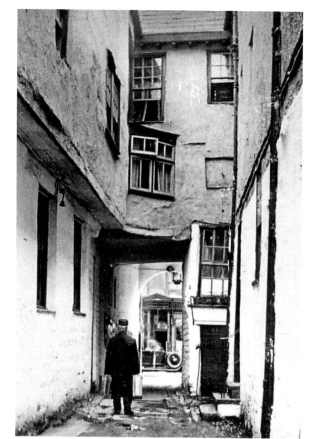

King's Arms Yard

In the old picture of the yard, looking out onto Stricklandgate, the gentleman is Mr Edward Woof, the King's Arms' porter seen carrying the bags of one of the hotel guests. Notice the old shoe scraper on the steps to the right, one of which is shown in the inset. At the far side of the road, behind the parked car, there is a doorway that is easily recognisable as the one in the centre of today's picture.

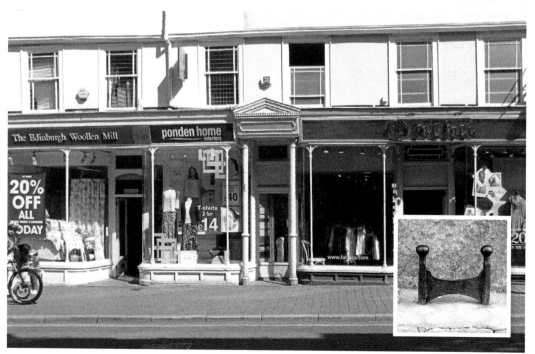

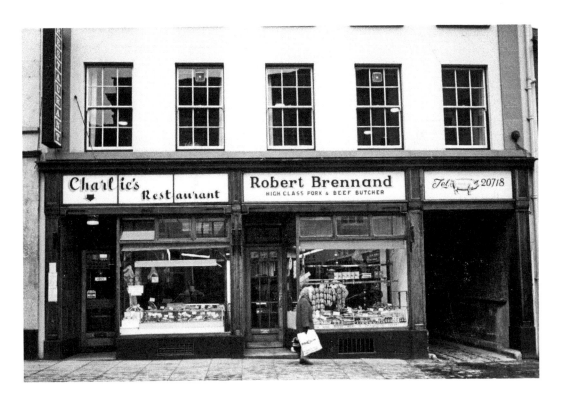

Brennand's

Established in 1912 at an earlier property in Kirkland, this old picture shows Robert Brennand's butcher's shop in Stricklandgate; sausage rolls and pies were made in the bakehouse at the rear of the premises. William Brennand, Robert's cousin, started his butcher's shop in Finkle Street in 1920. The archway to the right is now Wainwright's Yard. On the left, the doorway gives access to Charlie's Restaurant on the first floor. This later became a very popular Chinese restaurant and takeaway.

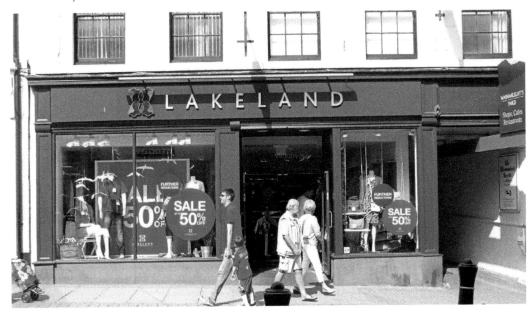

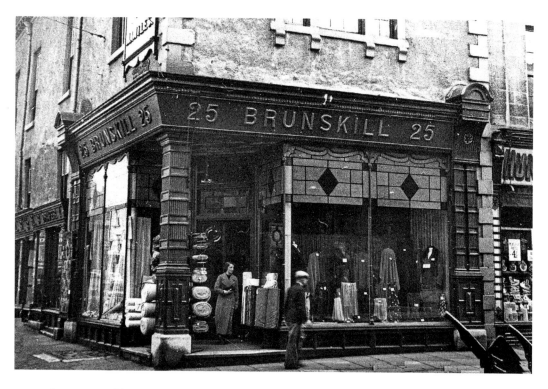

The Moot Hall/Brunskill's

Built in 1591 on this corner, the Moot Hall was used as the council meeting place until 1859, when the council moved to the White Hall. This in turn became the town hall. This building was, unfortunately, destroyed by a fire in 1969. As can be seen in the modern picture, when rebuilt its original Venetian window was reused and raised. Many older Kendalians will remember the property as Brunskill's Drapery Shop, which had begun trading here in the 1850s.

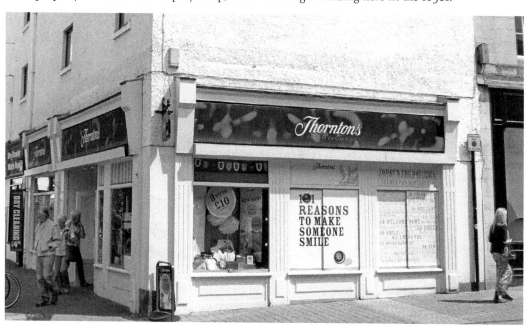

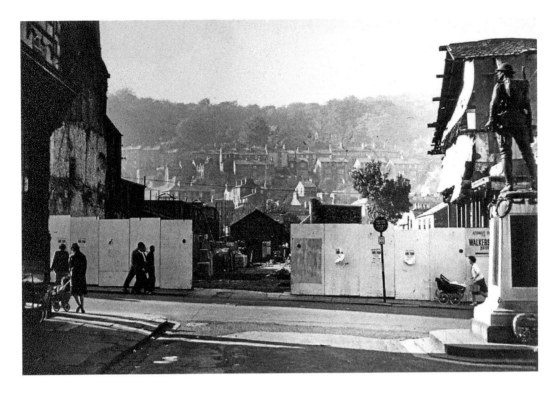

White Lion Yard, 1962

This was the scene in 1962 when the buildings, which used to be Townley & Taylor and Bird's shops, were removed to make way for the Co-op Wheatsheaf supermarket. The store was to be Kendal's first supermarket, which had an upstairs restaurant. Also lost in this development was the White Lion Yard. Most notable in the old picture is the war memorial on the right and Serpentine Woods in the distance, with the area of old Fellside in full view.

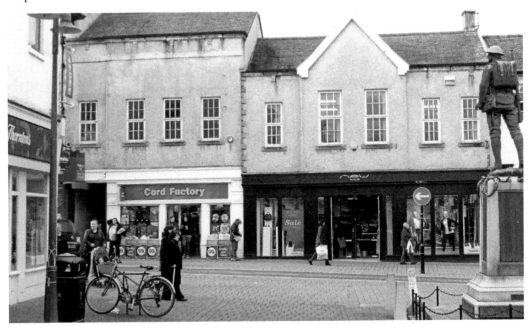

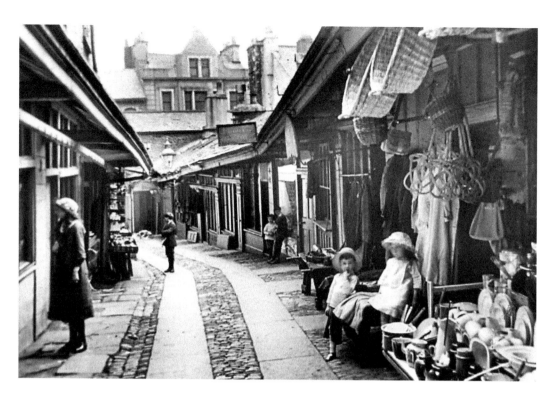

New Shambles

Here there is almost no difference between the two scenes. It is interesting that even the street lighting appears to be of a similar style in both pictures. Notice in the old picture the carpet beaters hanging on display outside. All these properties are owned and rented out to the various businesses by the Unitarian chapel, which is situated just off Branthwaite Brow. The blue-painted building in the background is that of The Works stationery shop.

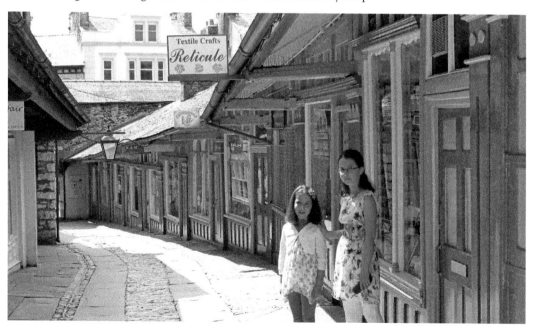

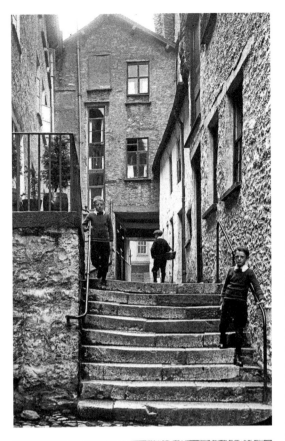

Old Police Yard

In 1817, a number of local tradesmen formed their own patrols to keep order in the town. Later, in 1832, the town's first police station was formed in this yard between Finkle Street and Market Place, consisting of a superintendent and three constables. The remains of the original police cells can still be found under some of the buildings on the left. At the bottom of the steps in Finkle Street was the town's first fire station and original post office. The yard, now merely a connection between two streets, has also in its time contained a solicitor, an accountant, a milliner's, a Citizens Advice Bureau and public toilets. As part of the fiftieth anniversary celebrations of Kendal Civic Society, they are planning to improve the yard by repainting, restoring the stonework and adding lighting. It is hoped that a mural by a local artist can also be part of the restoration.

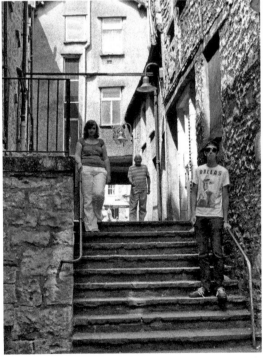

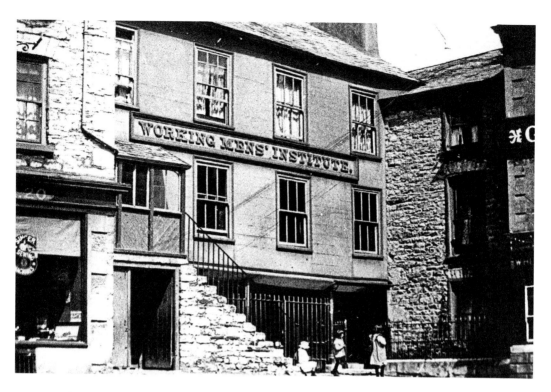

Working Men's Institute

Situated in the corner of Market Place, this building is often passed by without being given a second glance. Students of grammar would be interested in its misplaced apostrophe. It is said that John Wesley once preached from these steps when it was used as a chapel. It has in later years been used as a furniture storeroom, and on the ground floor the estate agency of Peill & Co. was established in 1980.

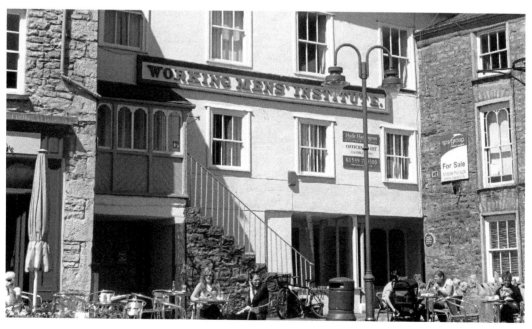

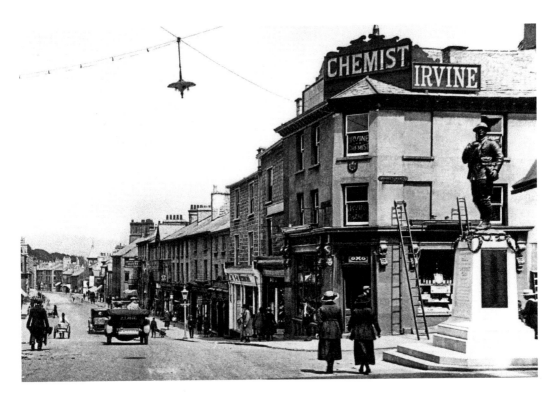

Stricklandgate

The old picture looking down Stricklandgate has a great deal of interesting aspects: firstly, notice the cables supporting the early electric street lighting, and the gas lamp just down the slope; secondly, the chemist's shop signs are on the roof of the building that later became Boon's Chemist and is now a men's clothing shop; thirdly, the Mercer's crest under the top floor window, which appears to have moved in the new picture. Most of the buildings at the Westmorland Shopping Centre have been altered.

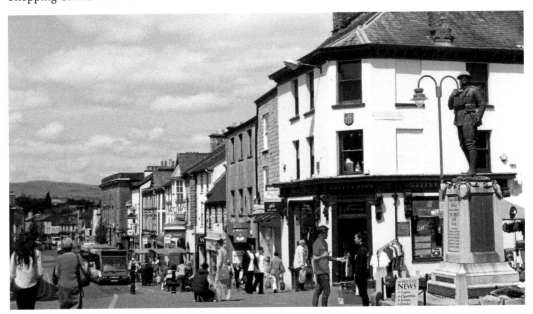

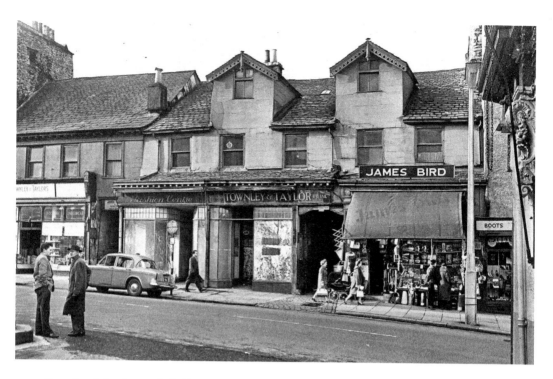

Townley & Taylor and Bird's

These two old shops were demolished in 1962. In the old picture, Townley & Taylor's windows were already whited out, the business having moved down the road to a property near the Westmorland Shopping Centre. Bird's ironmongers were still operating, with some of their goods on display outside on the pavement prior to their complete closure. The yard between the two shops was the White Lion Yard, which served the hotel of the same name.

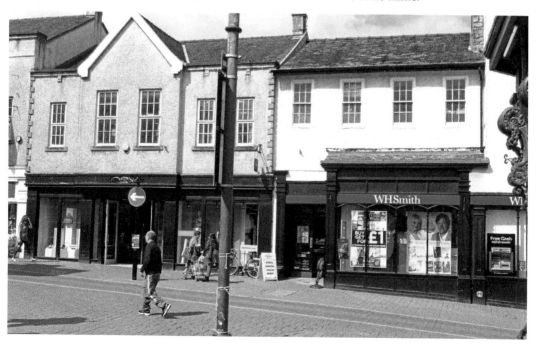

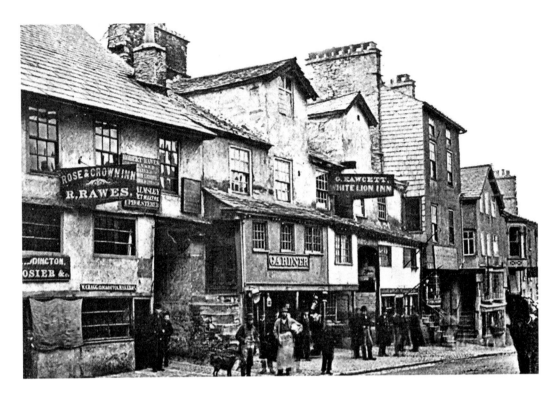

White Lion and Rose & Crown Inns

The building on the right, with the slated wall, is now part of WHSmith. The properties to the left, including the White Lion and Rose & Crown inns, have all been demolished. Notice in the old picture that there are two sets of steps either side of the entrance to Entry Lane, and another set near to Rose & Crown Yard. In today's picture, the doorway to WHSmith would have been the entrance to White Lion Yard.

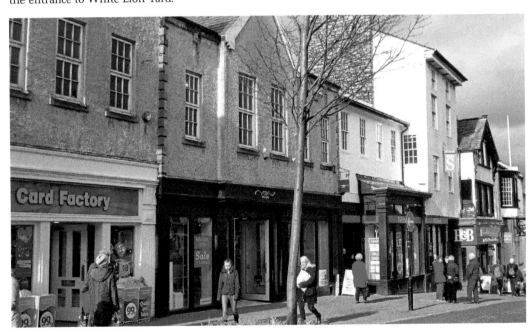

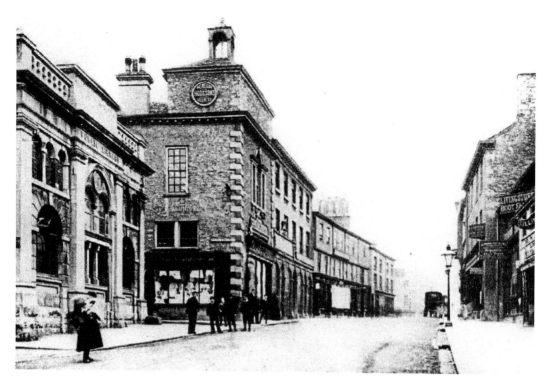

Moot Hall and Library

In the centre of the old picture is the site of the Moot Hall, which was Kendal's first town hall. The council moved from here to the White Hall in Highgate, which later became the new town hall. The building on the left was the old library before it moved to Stricklandgate and onto its present site. On the far right is the site of the White Lion hotel, and to the right of the street light is where today's Wainwright's Yard can be found.

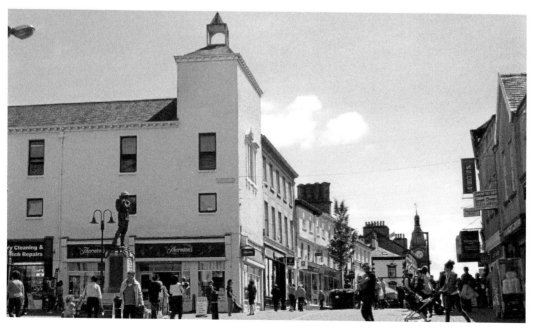

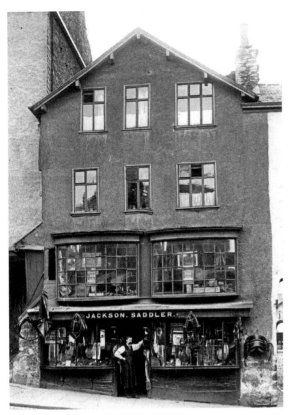

Jackson's

This property at No. 54 Stricklandgate
has been in use by many varied
businesses over the years. The earliest
on pictorial record, shown in the
old picture of around 1873, is that of
Jackson's saddlery shop. This building
was over four floors, the first two
being the shop and the top two the
living quarters. Notice in the old
picture the saddles hanging up outside
and the small stairway to the upper
floor of the shop. Also on the left is
the entrance to Entry Lane, while
on the right is the Woolpack Yard.
For many years, the property was
McCormack's furniture shop, then it
became Halfords and is now Holland
& Barrett's.

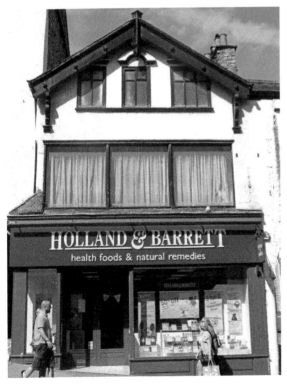

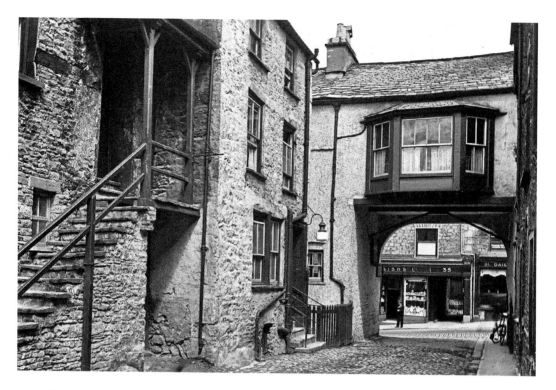

Woolpack Inn

This old view of the Woolpack Inn, from the rear, shows the entrance to the hotel up the steps under the white lamp; today's entrance has changed only slightly. The archway and large bay window are a prominent feature of the hotel from whichever side it is viewed. Very little of the original building remains today, but notice the old flagged stairway on the left leading to the upper floors, and the grocer's, Daish's Limited, under the archway across the street.

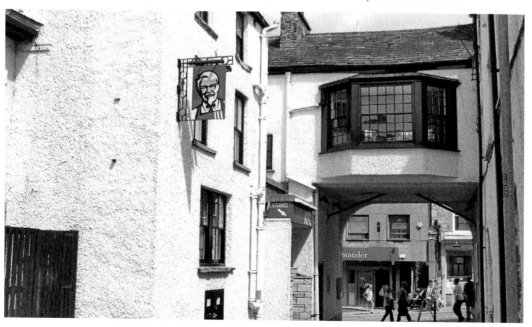

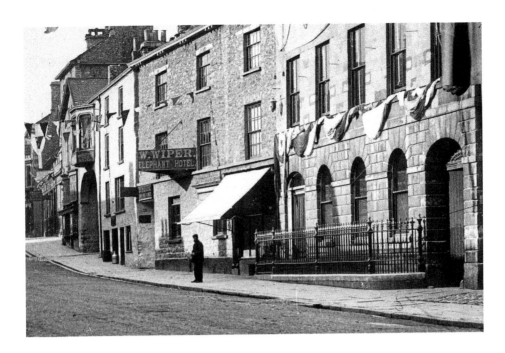

Elephant Yard

In the old picture, it would be difficult to find the yard if it were not for the large sign for the Elephant Hotel. The original yard is, in fact, to the left of the gentleman on the pavement, whereas today's yard is about 75 metres further down the street. The only thing that remains today is the front of The Woolpack Hotel. In the new picture, the far left pillar of Boots is the site of the old yard entrance.

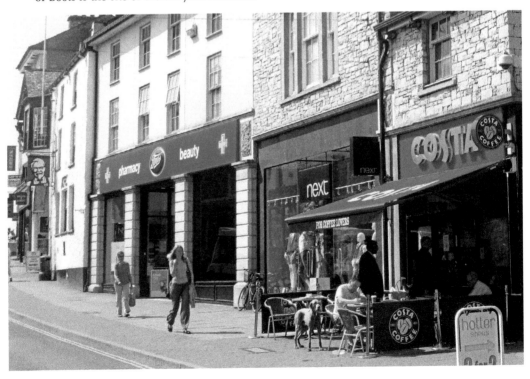

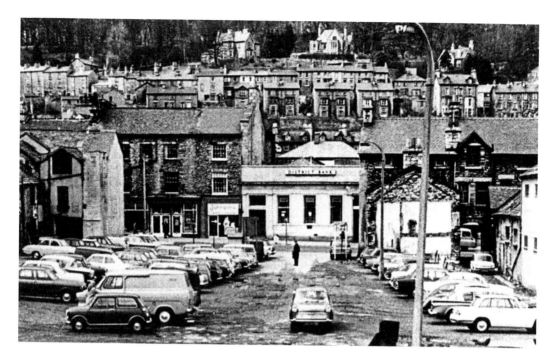

Stricklandgate Car Park

The modern picture is taken as close to the original as possible from inside the Westmorland Shopping Centre, which was built over the car park in 1980. Notice in the old picture the two business names of Johnsons The Cleaners on the left and District Bank in the centre. This bank later became NatWest and moved to the top of Elephant Yard. On the extreme right was Briggs' boot stores, which is now occupied by Thomas Cook.

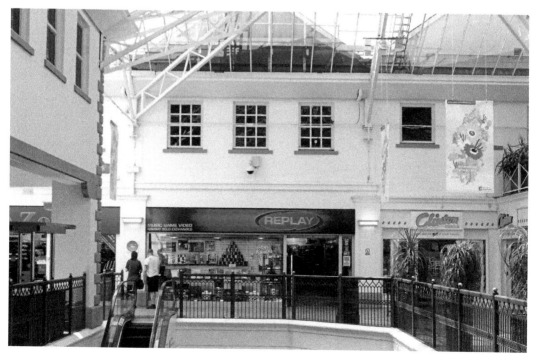

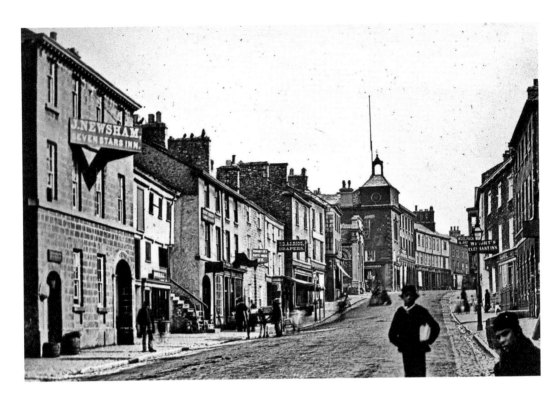

Seven Stars

In the old picture, the Seven Stars public house, shown on the left, was at one time owned by Whitwell Mark of the brewery in Highgate. It was demolished in 1989 during the construction of the Westmorland Shopping Centre. The archway to the left now leads to the small collection of shops in Blackhall Yard, which at one time contained the Labour Hall, Salvation Army Hall, and houses. As can be seen in today's picture, most of the property at the centre left is now totally changed.

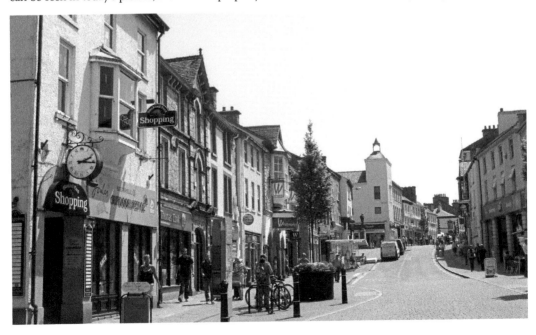

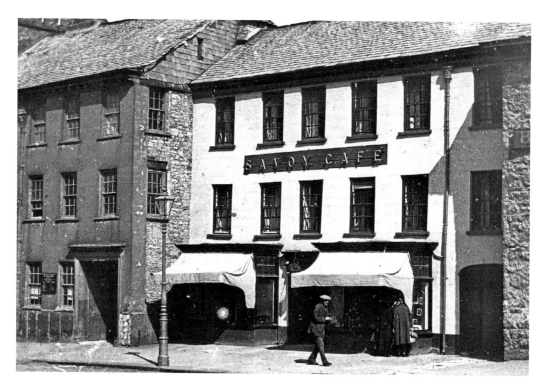

Savoy Café

The Savoy Café in Stricklandgate was, in its early days, Hogg's Photographic Studio, where many of Kendal's wonderful old pictures originated. After the café was demolished in 1968, it was resurrected as Lipton's supermarket, which also had a café on the first floor, accessed by a side door on the right. When the property was again demolished, a new structure arose from the rubble in the form of the well-known McDonald's, still continuing the café theme.

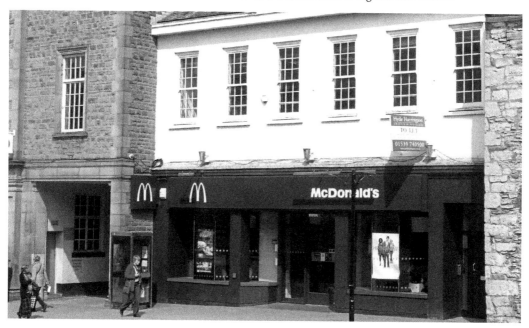

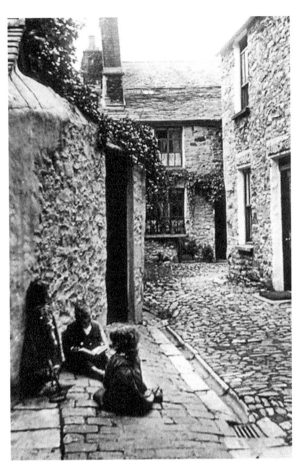

Noble's Yard

This old yard is typical of the way the Kendal yards used to be. The yards were named either after the business based in the yard, the name of the owner of the property, or an important person living there. This particular yard was named after Dr Samuel Noble, who lived and worked close by in Stricklandgate House from 1913 until his death in 1926. The park known locally as Noble's Rest was dedicated in his memory.

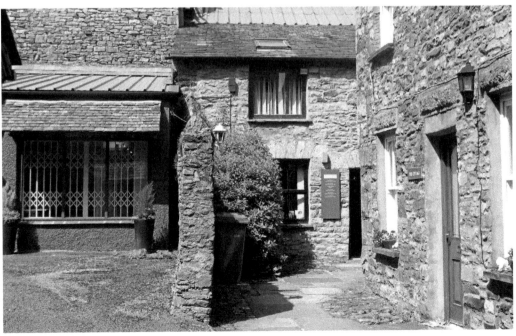

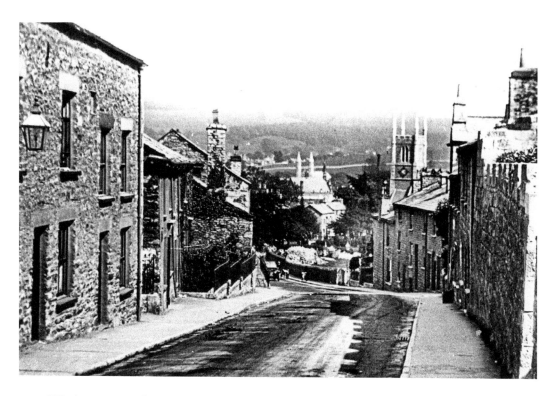

Windermere Road

The old picture was taken from the corner with Queen's Road, close to the site of the House of Correction. The cart further down the hill is near the entrance to the old workhouse. The date was before 1920 as the twin spires of St George's church on Castle Street can still be seen prominently in the centre. In today's picture, that same position is taken up with a view of the clock tower on the County Hall, built in 1939.

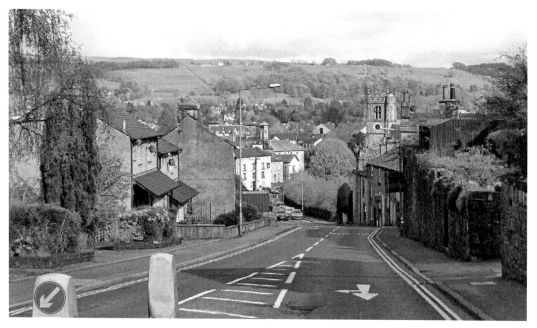

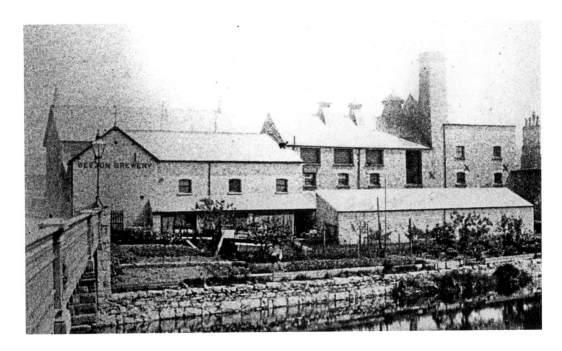

Beezon Brewery

The Beezon Road Brewery, making mineral and table waters, was established by Jonas Alexander in 1882 and extended into Sandes Avenue in 1906. The business was very successful, with an Alexander, namely Bruce Alexander, becoming mayor in 1936. The company continued trading until 1961, after which time the building on Sandes Avenue became part of the Provincial Insurance Company, while the Beezon Road site was demolished and rebuilt as a car showroom. The old picture was taken from the south side of Victoria Bridge.

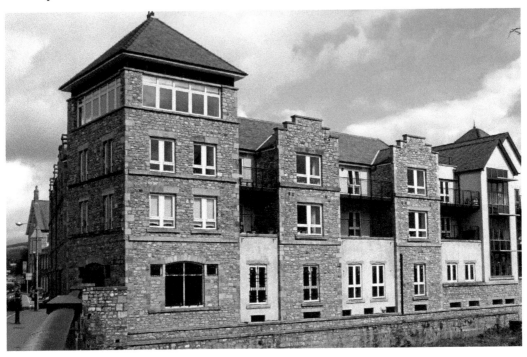

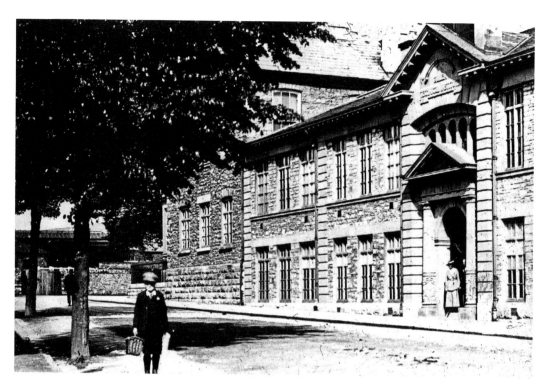

Allen Technical College

The college was built in 1912 and opened two years later. It was financed by a trust, set up by James Allen with a contribution of £10,000. The building had been part of Whitwell & Hargreaves' Wool Warehouse and the area used for storage was taken up by the college. This college was a forerunner of the very successful Kendal College on Milnthorpe Road and was mainly used by secondary school pupils and for further education by students who were already in employment.

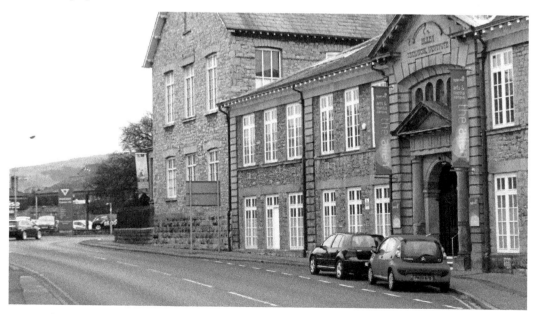

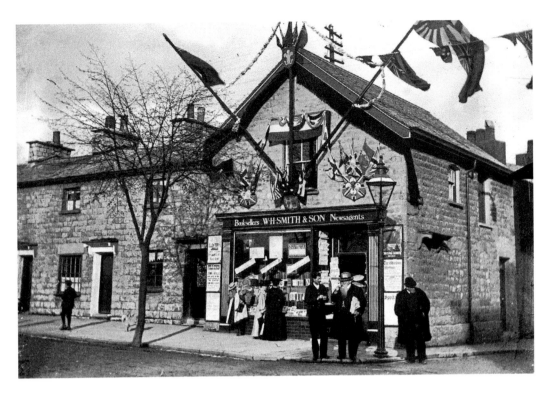

W. H. Smith & Son

This was not the first shop in Kendal to be owned by W. H. Smith & Son, as there was an earlier one situated at Kendal railway station. The poster to the left for Ellen Terry's Jubilee helps to date the picture as being taken around 1906; the flags were believed to celebrate a royal visit by Princess Christian to the town. Notice the books in the window for use in the shop's library.

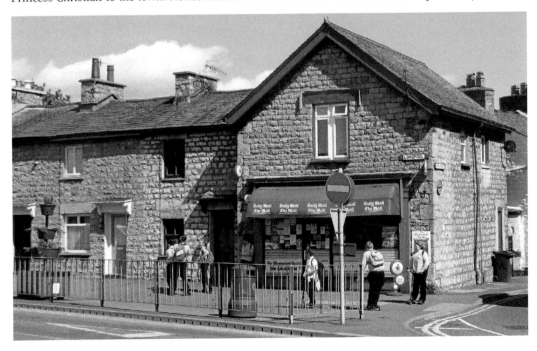

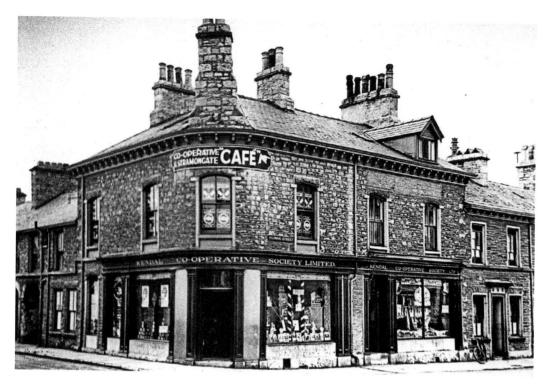

Wildman Street Co-op

The building on the corner of Wildman Street and Ann Street was one of the many Co-op shops established by the society in 1812; eventually they all suffered from supermarket competition. The head office was at Waterloo House in Finkle Street, which has now become a sports shop. The large advertising sign on the corner of the building is for the Co-op Café in Stramongate, which was a popular wedding reception venue in its day.

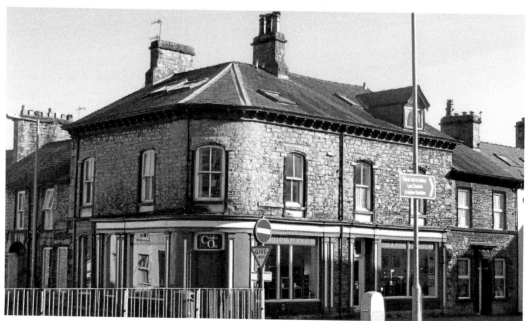

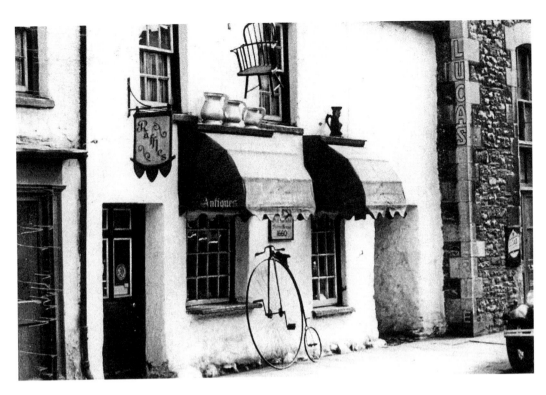

Sleddall Hall

This building dates from 1660, when this street was called Wildmans Gate. The first owner was Thomas Sleddall, one of Kendal's first aldermen and mayor in 1636. In 1887, to commemorate Queen Victoria's Jubilee, John Sleddall was the benefactor of the almshouse on Aynam Road that bears his name. This property is now an antique shop, with the remains of a spinning gallery at the rear. Notice, in the old picture, a penny farthing cycle and small chair hanging above the windows.

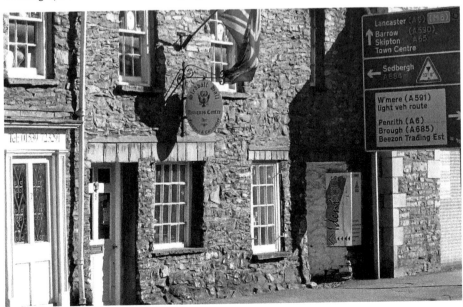

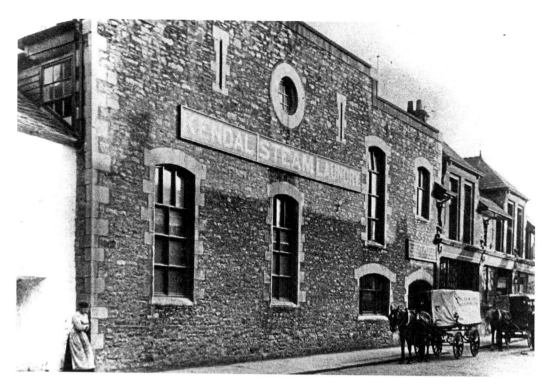

The Old Brewery

The building was originally one of Kendal's many breweries and the name can still be seen carved over the archway on the right. It was also at one time the Kendal Steam Laundry owned by Albert Pickles, and for many years Andrew Brown's auto electrical shop. Mr Brown had been an associate of Donald Campbell, the water speed record holder, who died on Coniston Water in 1967. The property is now used as the cycle retailer's, Askew Cycles.

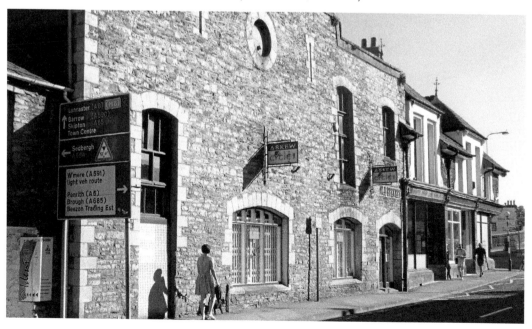

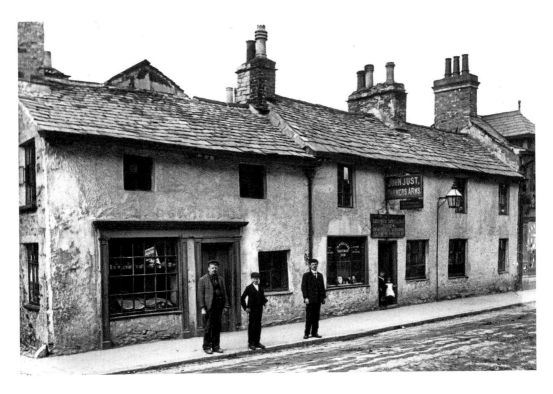

Farmers Arms

The Farmers Arms in Wildman Street (landlord John Just), viewed from the side of the Old Brewery, is now only a photographic memory, although Rawes Yard, on the left, still remains. On the site of the old public house, we have what remains of a long-established family business that was established in 1934 by Solomon Byrom. At one time the family had five shops in the town, and now a fourth-generation member of the family, Aaron, is helping to keep it going.

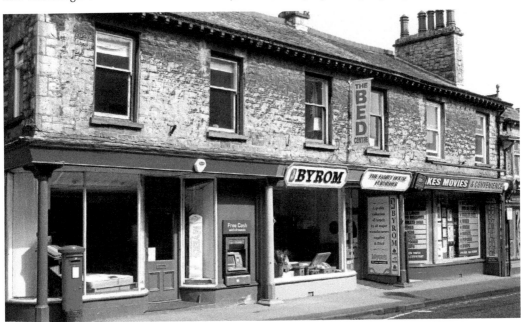

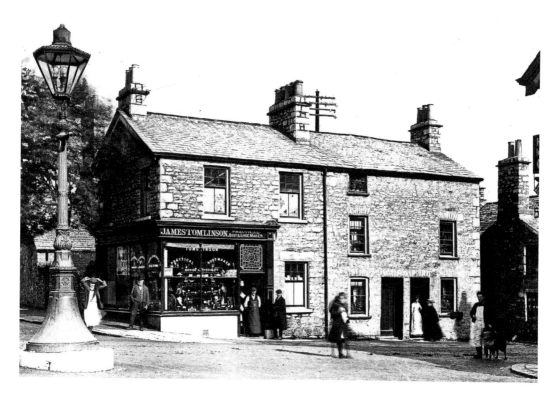

James Thomlinson's

The shop on the corner of Wildman Street and Beezon Road has been a catering equipment supplier since 1989. However, as can be seen in the old picture, it used to be James Thomlinson's boot and shoemaker's. Although the building has had minor changes to its appearance, most notable is the removal of the ornate street lamp in the centre of the road. To the right is Rawes Yard, named after Mr R. Rawes, the owner of a number of properties in the area.

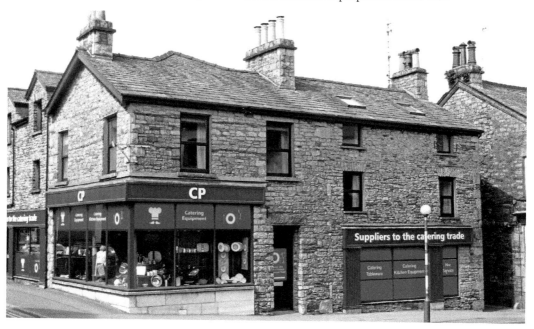

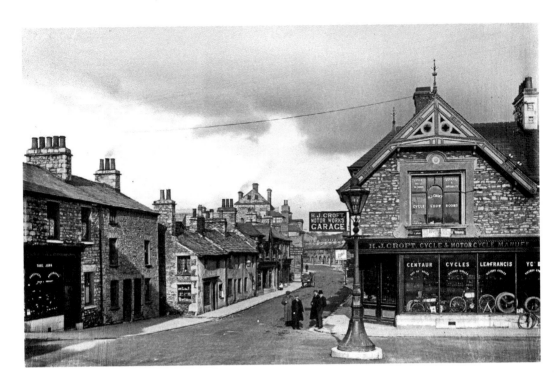

Wildman Street

A really wonderful view down Wildman Street, probably just after the Farmers Arms ceased trading, as the windows appear to be boarded up and the sign has gone. On the right is the business of H. J. Croft, who are selling cycles and motorcycles. Later, the business began selling cars and moved to larger premises in Highgate. The building in the centre left, with the gabled front, is still recognisable as a ladies' hairdressers, while the Castle Dairy is situated to the left of the old cart.

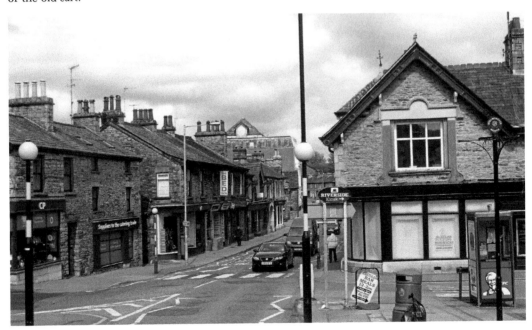

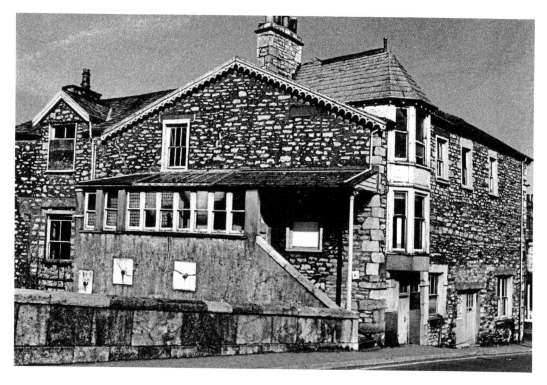

Riverside Hotel

This property on Stramongate Bridge was for many years owned by Charlie Pickles Wool Merchants and was acquired around 1970 by local builders Lowther & Dawson. The premises were used as joinery workshops until they were converted into the Riverside restaurant and hotel in 1983. Ten years later, the hotel was taken over by UAP Provincial and used as a training centre. Later it became part of the McDonald hotel group, and is now the Riverside Hotel & Leisure Club.

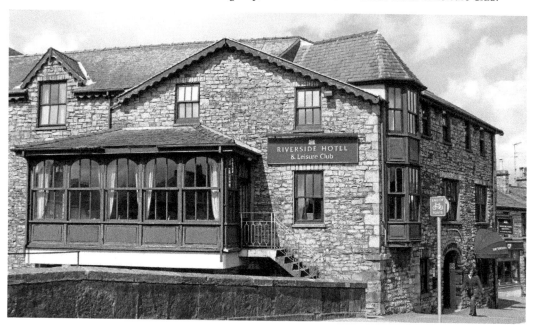

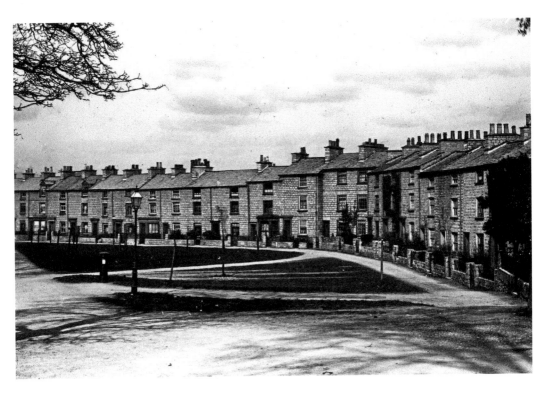

Castle Crescent

Situated behind St George's church, just off Castle Street and facing Gooseholme, this crescent was previously named Castle Buildings, and is a little older than the church. Before the church was built in 1840, the grassy area in front of the crescent was called Tenter Holme because of its use for drying cloth on tenter frames similar to those on Gooseholme. Notice in the old picture, centre left, the old gas lamp and pillar box that are no longer required today.

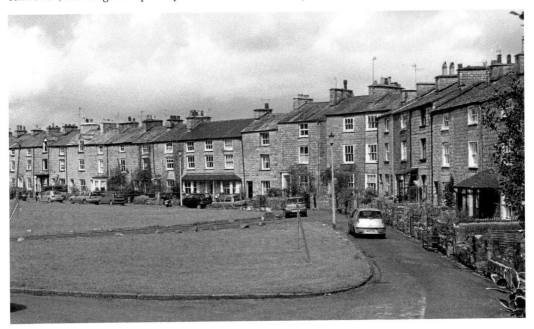

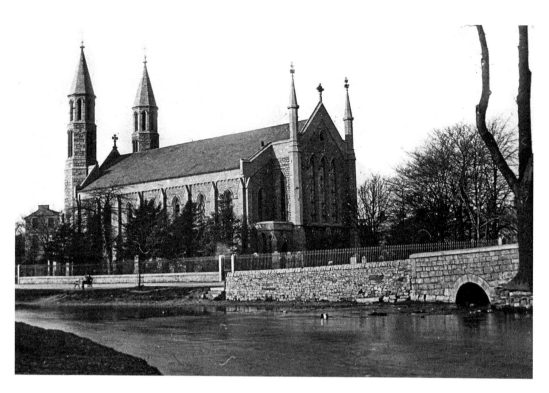

St George's Mill Race

Gooseholme used to be an island because of a weir near St George's church that went across to The Bridge Hotel. It was reached via a single footbridge from Melrose Place, before the second bridge that we know of today from New Road. The purpose of the mill race was to serve the mill that became Goodacre's carpet factory, and was filled in 1957 when the new weir and fish trap were constructed at Stramongate Bridge.

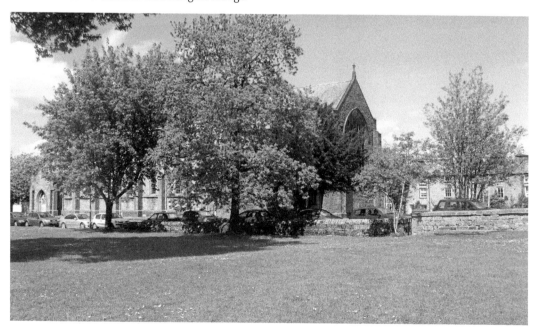

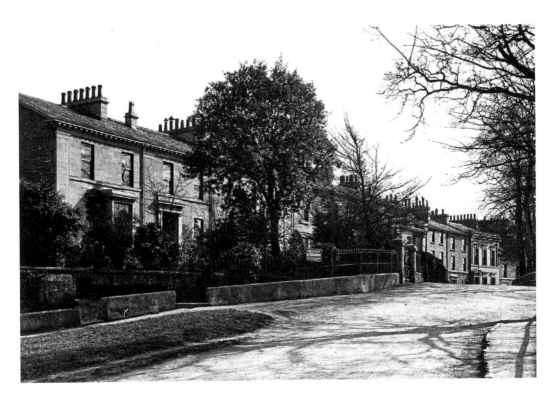

Thorny Hills

Before becoming Thorny Hills, this short stretch of road was named Kent Terrace, probably due to the River Kent flowing right in front of it. Local architects George and Francis Webster, who built the White Hall Assembly Rooms (now known as The Town Hall), designed and built this terrace of very individual styles in 1823. George lived here at No. 4 (the blue painted property). Both these pictures carry a notice announcing that this is a private road.

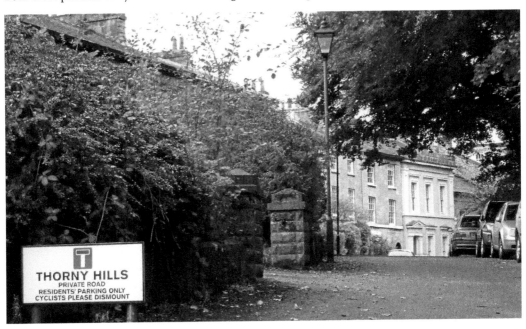

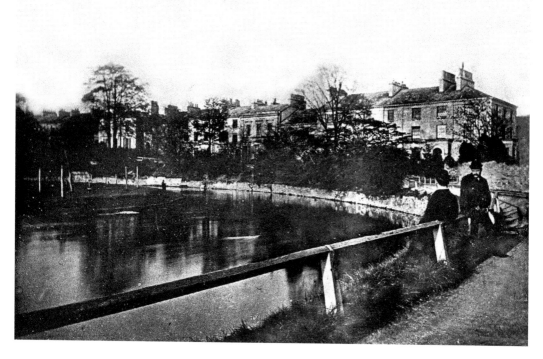

Thorny Hills and Mill Race

Here we have a view of the mill race near St George's church, rounding the corner at the end of Thorny Hills. As can be seen in today's picture, the water has long gone and the area has been used as the town's putting green since it moved here from Aynam Road in 1974. The building on the right was the second home of Kendal High School for Girls after having been established at Eller Bank on Sedbergh Road.

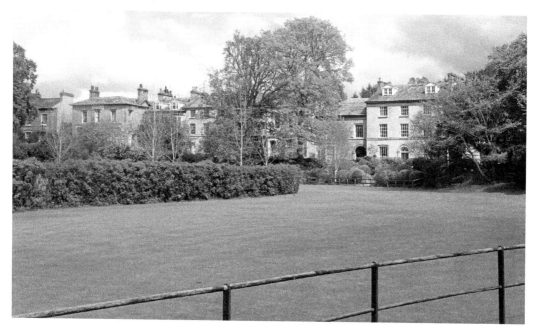

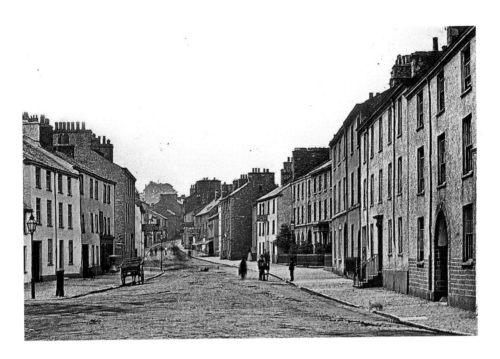

Stramongate School

The school was founded across the road as The Friends School in 1698, and moved to this site in 1772. John Dalton, the scientist, taught here for eight years from 1785. The entrance was through the archway to the left of the steps. The boys' school moved from this site to Windermere Road in 1932. The school later became Stramongate Primary School after the closure and amalgamation of both Castle Street and St George's schools. The main entrance is now from Sandes Avenue.

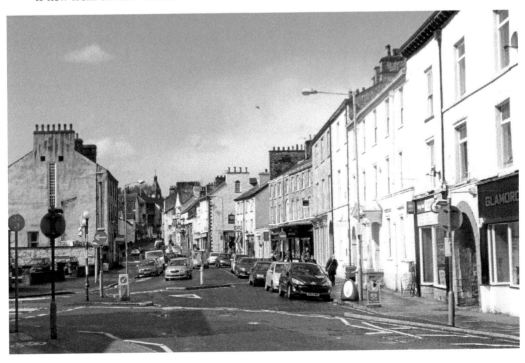

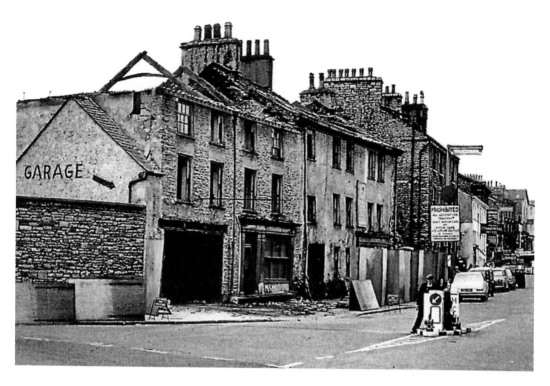

Stramongate Garage

This picture shows the demolition of the garage on the corner of Stramongate and New Road. It was used to provide garage parking space for Provincial Insurance and later became an extension to the main building. It is now used by a number of offices, including Radio Cumbria. The property beyond the white 'prohibited' sign is Stramongate House (a former doctors' surgery), while behind the hoarding is the Friends Meeting House, which previously had its entrance on New Road.

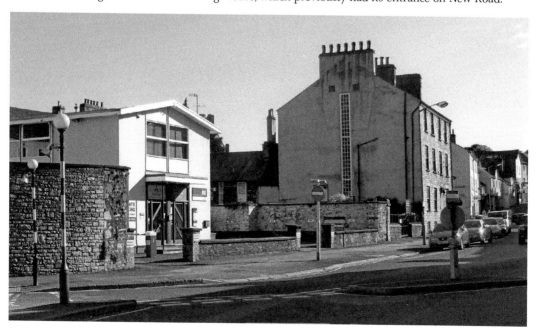

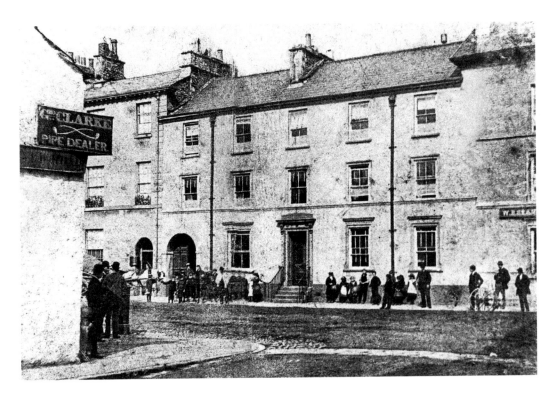

Grosvenor House

This property, at one time the Friends' Boarding School, opened in 1698. It was taken over in 1892 by Mr T. Mackereth who, assisted by his daughters, converted it into a first-class temperance hotel. This hotel, named The Grosvenor, was able to cater for more than 100 diners. After the hotel ceased trading, the property once again returned to education as Stramongate School until 1958. Towards the end of that year it became Grosvenor House Papers, and is now owned by Mullin Design.

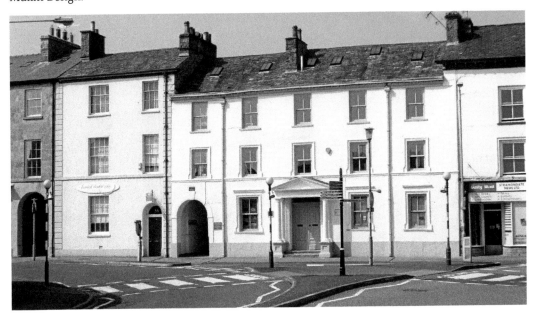

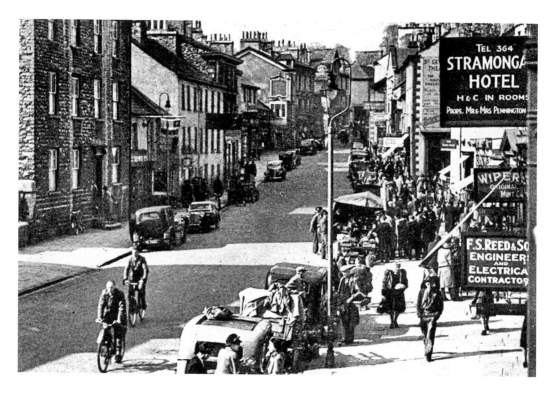

Stramongate, From Grosvenor House

The old picture depicts market day in Stramongate in the 1950s. The large gable-ended building in the centre, with the decorative panel on the side, was Bowman's fruiterers. The light-coloured building, centre left with the large black sign, is Webb's Commercial Hotel, which was removed to make way for Blackhall Road and the one-way system. The building on the right, with the dark cornerstones, is St George's Theatre. This was destroyed by a large fire in 1992.

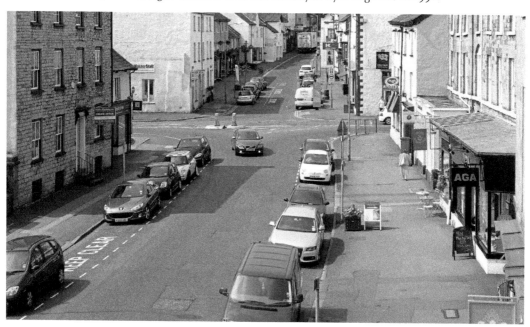

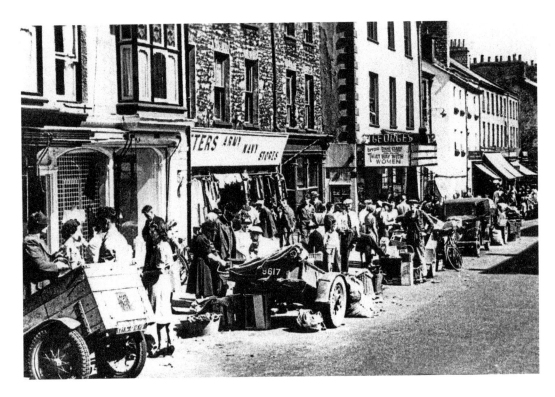

St George's Theatre

This is an old view of Stramongate Market when traders were still using carts to display their produce. Notice the cinema poster on St George's Theatre advertising the current showing of *That Way with Women*, starring Dane Clark. The film was made in 1947, which helps date the picture. Originally used as a theatre, it was later converted into a cinema and finally a bingo hall until it was destroyed by fire in 1992.

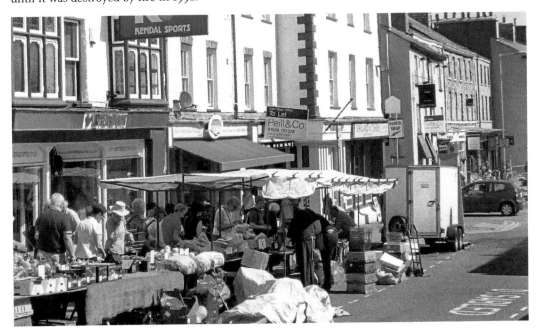

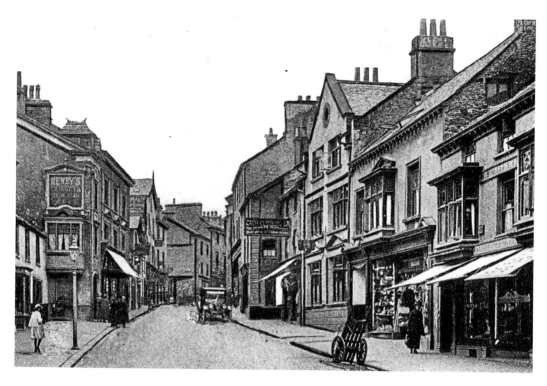

Masons Arms

The Masons Arms in Stramongate is believed to be so-named because it was used as a meeting place for the Freemasons in the 1830s. The masons' meetings were later held in part of St George's Theatre building, but after a disastrous fire they were transferred to their present site on Station Road. The public house is unusual in that it has no entrance onto Stramongate, but entry is gained by use of a yard at the side.

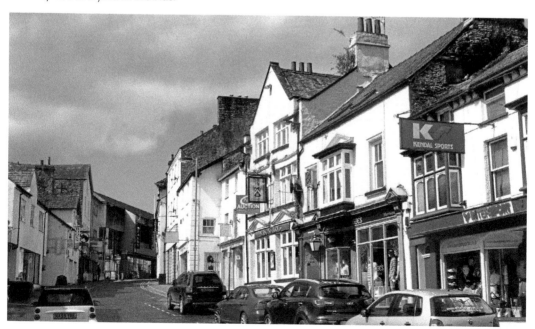

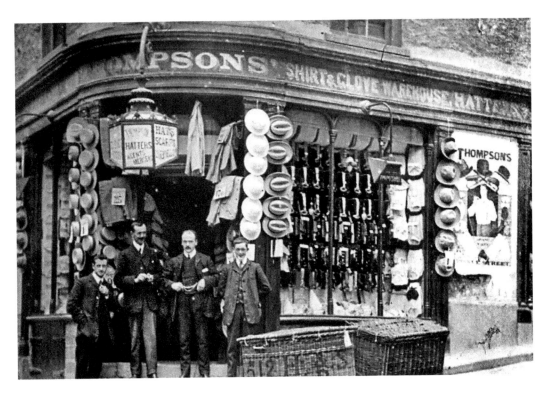

R. W. & T. K. Thompson

For many years, this shop on the corner of Finkle Street and Branthwaite Brow was Thompson's gentlemens' outfitters; on careful examination of the upper floor windows the name 'Thompson' can still be seen etched into the glass. To many of today's Kendalians, it will be well remembered as O'Loughlin's toy shop before it once again returned to its earlier trading status. The old picture shows the shop with many of its goods hanging outside – also notice the ornate lamp over the door.

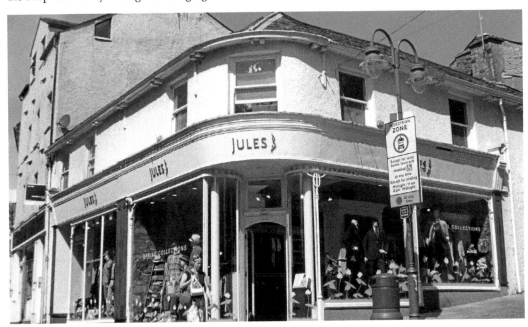

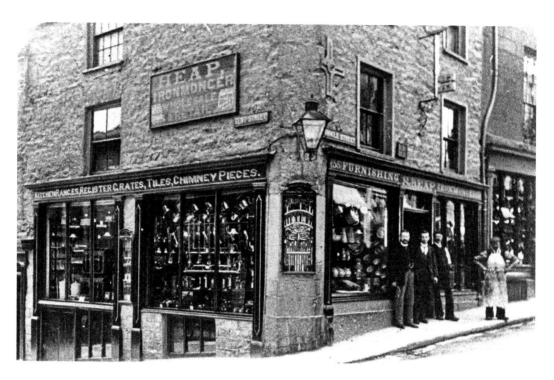

Heap's

This picture, taken on the corner of Kent Street and Finkle Street, shows Heap's ironmonger's shop with its distinctive key trade sign over the doorway. The property has been home to a number of businesses over the years, including the Electricity Board shop. It later became part of Musgroves' (which suffered a disastrous fire in 1958) and then J. R. Taylor's, before its present owners, Beales, took over. The Finkle Street buildings contained the site of one of Kendal's early post offices.

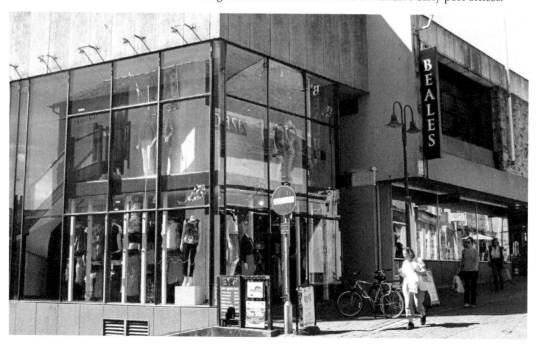

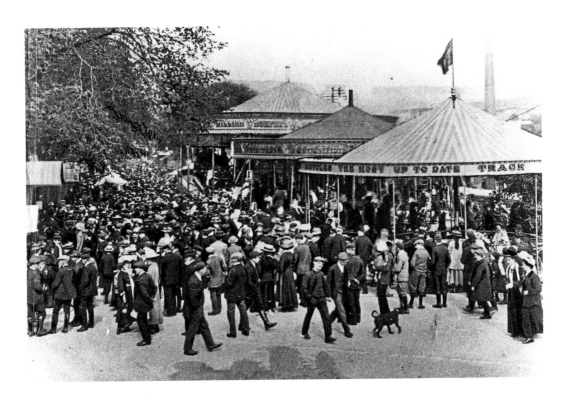

New Road Fair

The fair on New Road is held twice a year, usually in May and November; there is now an additional fair held in September during the time of the Kendal Torchlight Procession. The attractions used to go down to the edge of the river and across the road near to St George's Catholic church. The stalls and rides were extremely decorative and brightly coloured in the past, but nowadays appear to be a little drab in comparison.

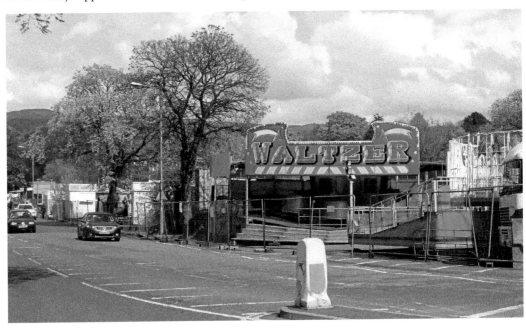

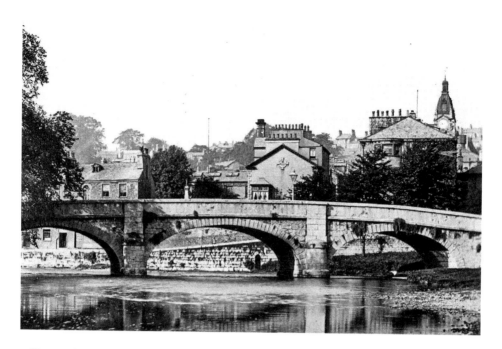

Miller Bridge

This bridge was originally built as a wooden structure, but it was rebuilt in stone in 1743, after it had been destroyed a number of times by floods. This even newer bridge, designed by local architect Francis Webster, was built in 1818 to serve the new Kendal canal terminus that opened a year later. The canal head consisted of wharves, warehouses, stables and cottages. The inset image shows the south-facing date stone on the bridge, which translates from the Roman numerals as 1818.

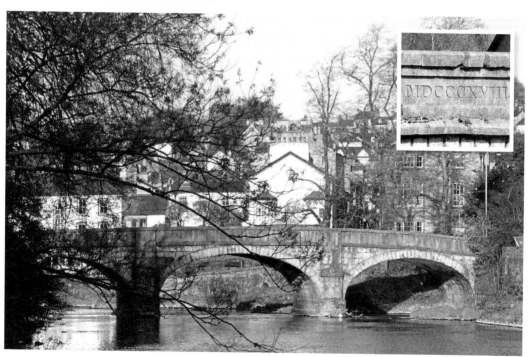

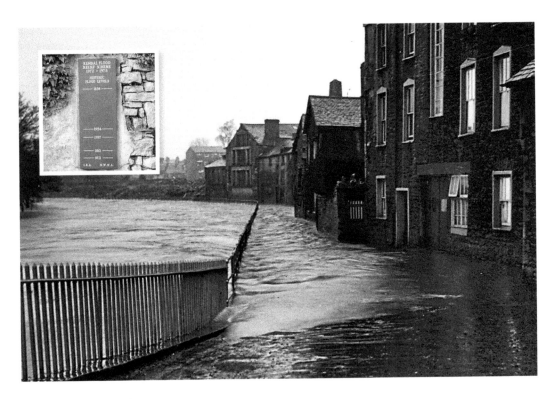

Waterside Flood, 1968

During the mid-1970s, a much-needed flood relief scheme, which widened the river at Miller Close and lowered stretches of the riverbed, saved the town from what had become a regular occurrence (see inset). There are many old pictures of past disasters that occurred in Ann Street, Wildman Street, Stramongate, Victoria Bridge and Milnthorpe Road. The worst always seemed to happen to the properties on Waterside and Aynam Road, where the water got into the cellars.

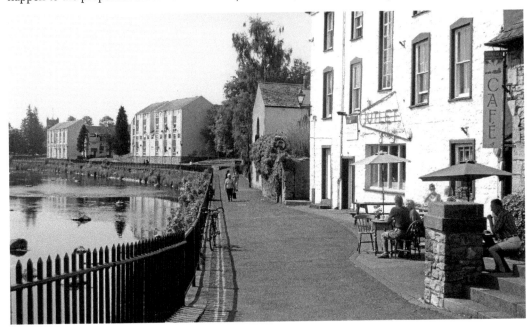

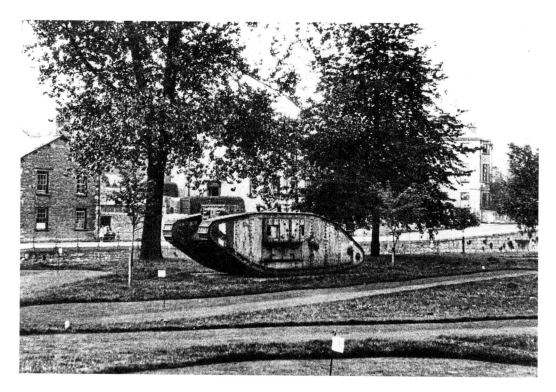

Aynam Road Tank

The tank on Aynam Road was a redundant First World War Lincoln Mark IV, built in 1917 and presented to the town by the war office. It was on display until 1939, when it was scrapped to make armaments for the Second World War. The small, white marker flags are evidence that this area was once used as a putting green. In the 1970s, as a result of the flood relief scheme that widened the river, the green was transferred to a new site on Gooseholme.

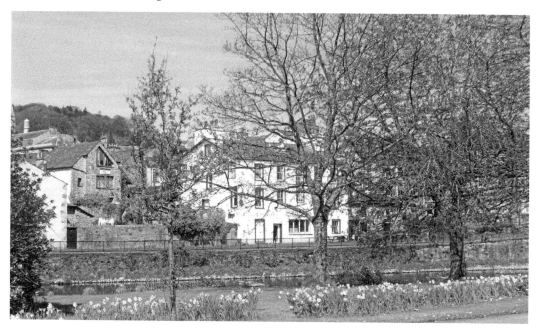

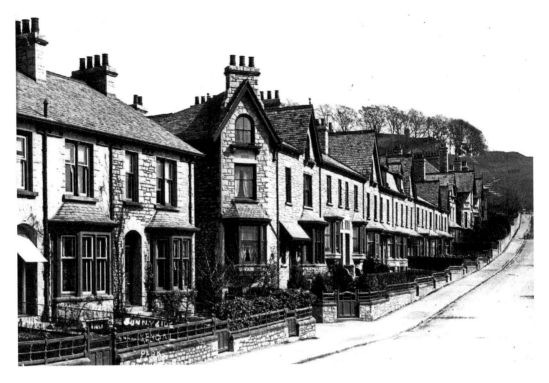

Sunnyside

In both these pictures, taken from the last canal bridge before Canal Head, the trees that are on Kendal Castle Hill can be seen. Opposite the aptly named Sunnyside, due to its south-facing aspect, is Fletcher Park. Here, one can find an amazing wooden sculpture by craftsman Andy Levy; it has been called *Katherine Parr Throne*. It was carved onto the stump of a 100-year-old beech tree, which came down during high winds in 2011.

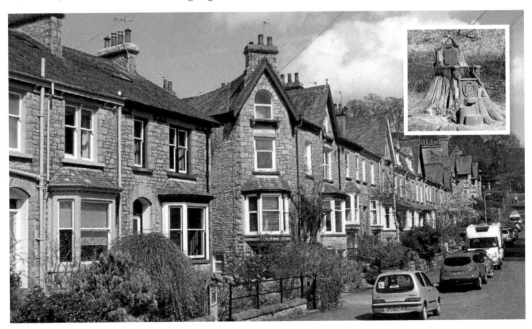

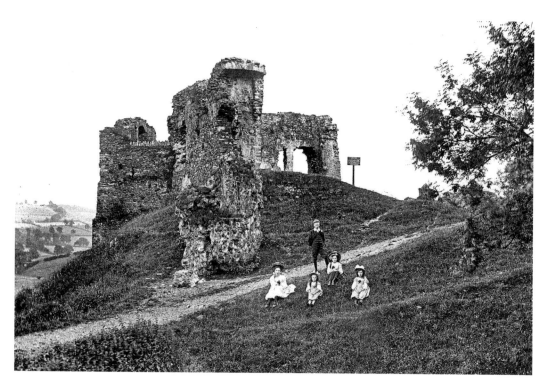

Kendal Castle

These pictures, taken from the outer area looking towards the entrance, show the town's second castle (the first one having been built at Castle Howe in the eleventh century). Nowadays, a feature in this area is the castle beacon, which was first lit on 1 January 1993 to commemorate the UK joining the European Union. This was also around the time that Kendal was twinned with Rinteln in Germany. The beacon was lit again during the celebrations of the new millennium.

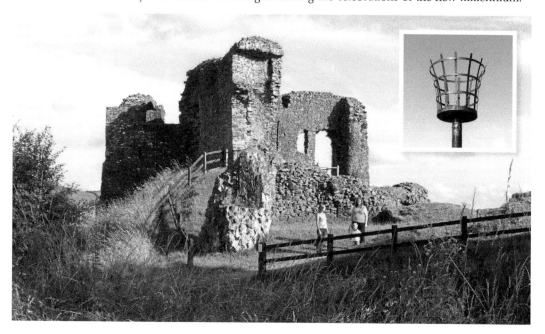

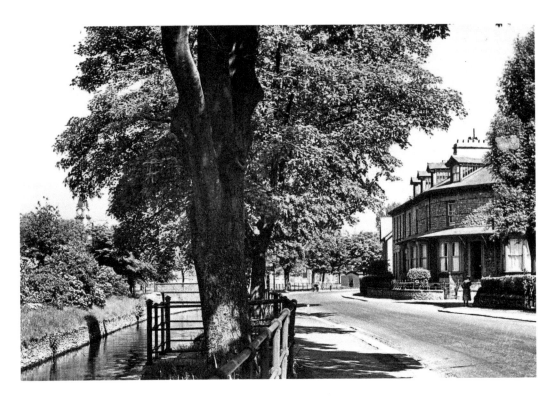

Aynam Road

The old picture of Aynam Road, with the entrance to Parr Street on the right, shows on the left the ending of the stretch of water known as the mill race, which had begun its journey outside St George's church on Gooseholme. Close to the left side of the tree trunk can be seen the old footbridge crossing the river to Waterside. In the modern-day picture, the town hall clock tower is obscured by foliage.

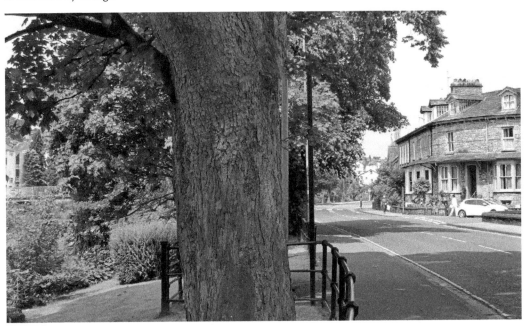

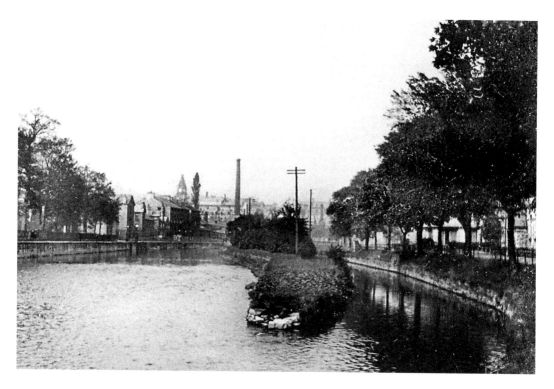

Aynam Road Mill Race

Further along Aynam Road, just on the bend in the old picture, can be clearly seen the end of the mill race with Wilkinson's organ works just visible on the extreme right. All the old buildings on the left, including the lodging house, which is just visible below the town hall clock tower, were replaced in 1969 during the Waterside redevelopment. Also in this area we can see the sets of steps leading down to the river, which were used for washing the wool.

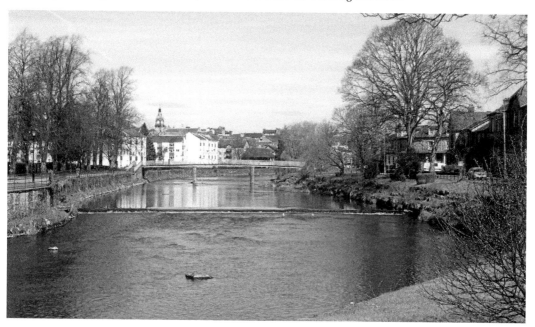

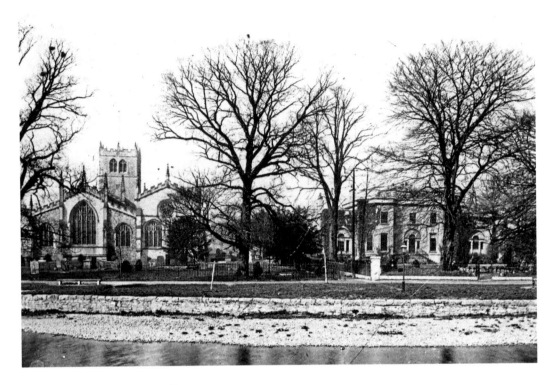

Parish Church and Abbot Hall

In this early spring view from across the River Kent, these two important buildings stand together in the oldest part of Kendal. It is amazing to think that the art gallery is some 560 years younger than the church, which is not even the oldest religious building in the town (see page 15). The church tower contains ten swinging bells plus an electric sanctus bell, while the gallery has ten rooms and contains over 4,000 works of art.

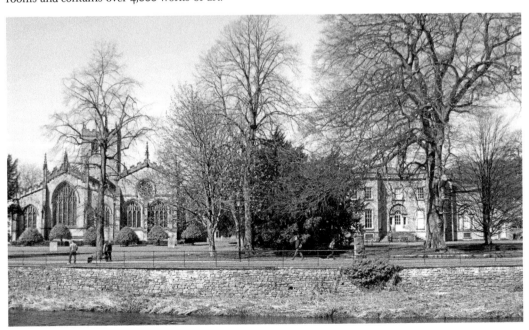

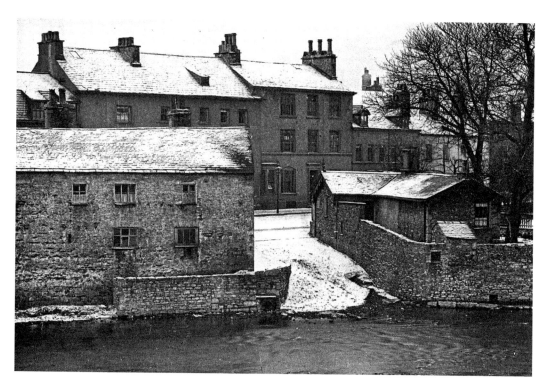

The Old Ford

There is not much with which to compare these two pictures, but close inspection would find, in the top left, the dormer windows on Youdell's Art Shop and, in the right foreground, the access to the ford. The buildings on the left are the Malt Kiln Cottages with the Glebe Cottage on the right. In today's picture can be seen the high archway into the sheltered housing and the newly constructed apartments on the right.

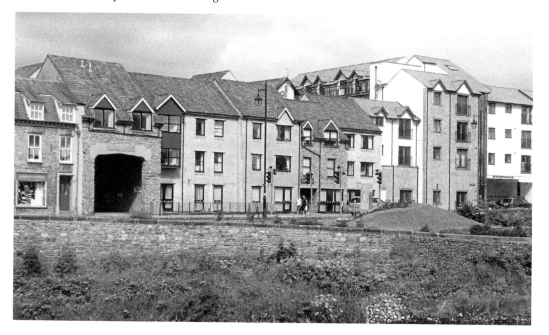

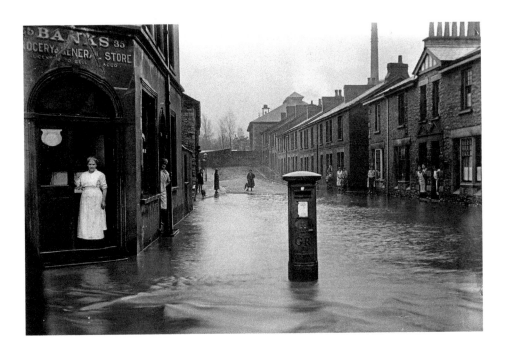

Nether Street Flood

Here we have another picture of flooding in Kendal, this time taken in 1927 at Nether Street, where the postbox appears to be standing in the road. The residents seem to be posing for the photographer. For many years, the carpet shop on the left was Cumbria Stores Spar shop. The large building at the top of the street (now used by Norweb) and the chimney were part of the gasworks on Parkside Road. The chimney was demolished in 1969.

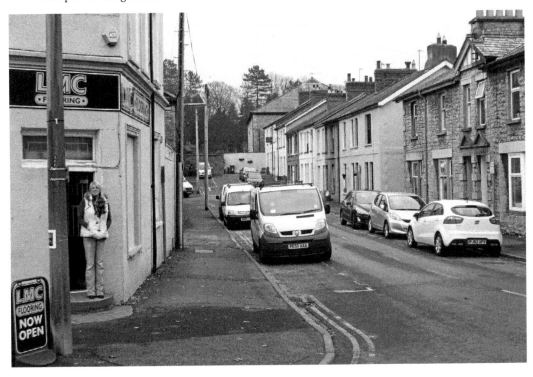

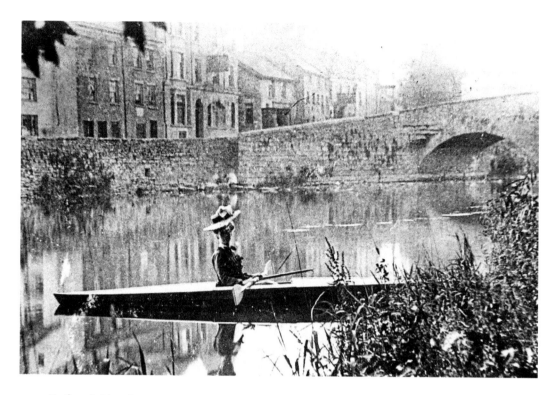

Nether Bridge Canoe

This scene is viewed from the K Village, where the water is deeper and mirror smooth due to the weir further downstream, near to the Old Romney Footbridge. The lady in the canoe was the daughter of Harold Hill Day, the owner of Day's Foundry, established in 1893 at Canal Head South. Notice, behind Miss Day's canoe, the arched doorway of the former Cock & Dolphin public house, which, after its closure in 2012, was carefully restored and renovated by local builders Russell Armer.

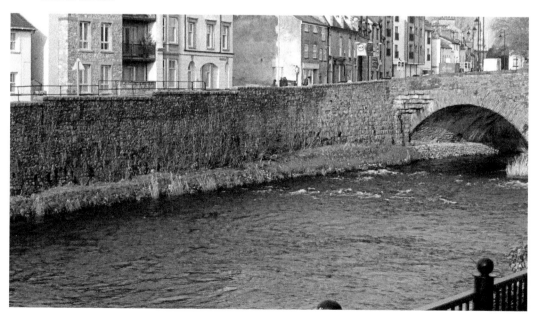

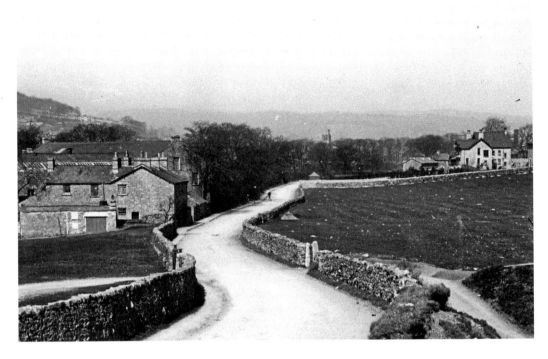

Low Mills

Dating from around 1840, the Low Mills buildings, on the left in the old picture, are still recognisable in today's photograph, just behind the street light. The large building on the right was a former home of the Crabtree family and is now Levens Close. The smaller houses to its left are Nos 2–10 Natland Road, with the toll house beyond. In the centre distance the bell tower of Kendal parish church can be seen.

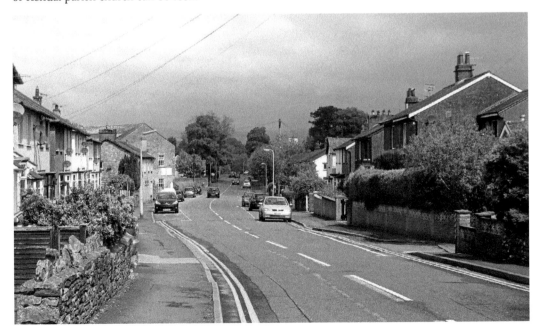